The Fulgoroidea, Or Lanternflies Of Trinidad And Adjacent Parts Of South America

Ronald Gordon Fennah

PROCEEDINGS OF THE UNITED STATES NATIONAL MUSEUM

issued   *by the*

SMITHSONIAN INSTITUTION
U. S. NATIONAL MUSEUM

| Vol. 95 | Washington: 1945 | No. 3184 |

THE FULGOROIDEA, OR LANTERNFLIES, OF TRINIDAD AND ADJACENT PARTS OF SOUTH AMERICA

By R. G. FENNAH

THE major portion of the material with which the present report is concerned was collected in Trinidad by the writer partly during occasional visits dating from 1937 but chiefly between April 1942 and March 1943. To this was added a small but very interesting group from the collection of the Imperial College of Tropical Agriculture, built up since 1933, and a few specimens in an imperfect condition from an older collection originally belonging to the former Imperial Department of Agriculture for the British West Indies. Types, paratypes, or representative material of species discussed have been deposited in the United States National Museum (U.S.N.M.) and the British Museum of Natural History (B.M.N.H.) as stated under each. Certain paratypes have also been placed in the Museum of Comparative Zoology, Cambridge, Mass., and in the collection of the Imperial College of Tropical Agriculture, Trinidad.

The warmest thanks of the writer are due to Dr. A. M. Adamson, professor of zoology at the Imperial College of Tropical Agriculture, for his ready offer of the material in his charge for the present study, and to Dr. E. McC. Callan, lecturer in zoology, for gifts of specimens from time to time. For his constant assistance in the naming of species the writer is deeply indebted to W. E. China, of the British Museum. Mr. China has examined more than half the species and has commented on notes and drawings submitted to him from time to time, and his remarks are added below the species to which they refer.

In this report the terms *vertex* and *frons* are retained as a matter of convenience; there is good reason to believe that the former represents the basal part of the orthopteroid vertex, while the latter, as far as the frontoclypeal suture, represents the anterior portion of the vertex lying basad of the median ocellus. The lateral carinae of the frons are the carinae lying between the median carina and the lateral margins; the lateral carinae of the pronotal disk lie between the middle line and the apparent edge, seen in dorsal view, between the eye and the tegula on each side. In the tegmina the *apical line* is the first transverse line of cross veins basad of the apical margin; the *nodal line* is the shortest transverse line between the nodal area, near the apex of Sc, and the apex of the clavus. In the female genitalia the third pair of valvulae, which compose the ovipositor sheath in forms with a complete ovipositor, are termed *lateral styles* where the ovipositor is incomplete.

In the descriptions that follow, the characters of the genitalia are considered in some detail, irrespective of sex. Although those afforded by the female genitalia are usually not so conspicuous as their counterparts in the male, they have in many cases equally high diagnostic value, and in the writer's opinion are of importance in indicating the relationship of genera. Whenever possible the form of the egg has been described; it is not yet certain whether the variations observed are of specific or of generic value. In the case of the compact Antillean flatid genera *Antillormenis* and *Ilesia* it is definitely established that the shape of the egg does not vary within the genus. In the Trinidadian Flatidae the difficulty is not to discover differences between the eggs of obviously different genera, but to find eggs that are alike within any supposedly homogeneous genus.

The classification used herein follows that adopted by Muir (Ann. Mag. Nat. Hist., ser. 10, vol. 6, pp. 461–478, 1930). For the rapid determination of genera the student is referred to keys given by Metcalf (Bull. Mus. Comp. Zool., vol. 82, No. 5, 1938), which although relating to Central America are sufficiently applicable to genera occurring in Trinidad; in the same work may be found an extensive bibliography of American Fulgoroidea. The figures that illustrate the present paper have been drawn by the writer.

In Trinidad only a very limited amount of collecting has so far been done in this group, but sufficient evidence is already available to prove that the fulgoroid fauna of the island is continental and has a close affinity to that of the Brazilian subregion, though being relatively impoverished. So far no representatives of the families Tettigometridae, Achilixiidae, or Lophopidae have been recorded in Trinidad, although species of all occur in South America. Three families found in Trinidad (Fulgoridae, Dictyopharidae, and Nogodinidae) are absent from the Lesser Antilles, which lie to the north. (The references to Lesser Antillean Dictyopharidae in literature are all due to misinterpretation of tropiduchid genera.) The genera found in Trinidad, excluding genera described below, about the distribution of which little is known, also occur on the mainland; in contrast to this comparatively few genera are common to Trinidad and the Lesser Antilles, and include *Oliarus*, *Pintalia*, *Bothriocera* (Cixiidae), *Burnilia*, *Saccharosydne*, *Peregrinus*, *Sogata*, *Delphacodes* (Delphacidae), *Neocenchrea*, *Cedusa*, *Patara*, *Otiocerus* (Derbidae), *Catonia* (Achilidae), *Euhyloptera*, *Flatoidinus* (Flatidae), *Acanalonia* (Acanaloniidae), and *Thionia* (Issidae). That the Lesser Antillean fulgoroid fauna is not in turn to be regarded as a greatly impoverished Trinidadian fauna is shown by the number of genera that do not appear to occur in Trinidad, such as *Cyphoceratops*, *Tangidia* (Tropiduchidae), *Quilessa*, *Prosotropis* (Kinnaridae), *Cionoderus* (Achilidae), *Scarposa*, *Antillormenis*, and *Ilesia* (Flatidae).

Occasional specimens of most fulgoroid species may be found resting or feeding on crops that have been planted in cultivations encroaching on their natural habitat, and most of these are of economic importance only as possible vectors of disease. The most serious pest species is the delphacid *Peregrinus maidis* (Ashmead), which has been shown to be a local vector of stripe disease of maize (H. R. Briton-Jones and R. E. D. Baker, Tropical Agriculture, vol. 10, Nos. 5 and 8, 1933); another species of the same family, *Saccharosydne saccharivora* (Westwood), is quite common on sugarcane but in Trinidad does not appear to develop in great numbers. The cixiid *Paramyndus cocois* (described below) occurs in the adult stage in abundance on the lower surface of leaves of coconut, where many may be found killed by fungus; the nymphal stages are subterranean. This insect forms an interesting parallel to *Euryphlepsia cocois* Muir, which infests coconuts in a similar manner in the south Pacific. *Paramyndus* has been collected on sugarcane and Guatemala grass and is not obligately restricted in its choice of host. Among pests of minor importance may be listed the dictyopharid species *Taosa herbida* (Walker) and *Retiala viridis* (described below), which for short periods may be abundant on coffee, a crop also attacked by the ever-present flatids *Flatormenis squamulosa* (Fowler), *Epormenis fuliginosa* (Fennah), and *Ormenis antoniae* Melichar, which occur on the plant in all stages. The last-named species is common also on the leaves and stems of mango, the large squat nymph apparently preferring the former and the adult the latter situation. In forested areas the kinnarid *Bytrois nemoralis* (described below) often feeds in the adult stage on the leaves of cacao, which is also attacked over a wider area by *Epormenis unimaculata* (Fennah) and the acanaloniids *Acanalonia theobromae* and *A. umbellicauda* (described below). The former of these has been taken in abundance on *Flacourtia*, and in lesser numbers on the ornamental *Caesalpinia pulcherrima*, with all stages occurring on the stems of the host. *Poekilloptera phalaenoides* (Linnaeus) (Flatidae) is common in all stages on saman (*Samanea*), where it is restricted to branches that are dying back. An otherwise uninfested tree often bears one or two small branches that are heavily encrusted with the white flocculence laid over the row of inserted eggs or exuded from the thoracic and abdominal glands of the nymph. It is apparently not possible to rear this species unless twigs in a condition of senescence (and not artificially induced moribundity) are provided as food; fresh healthy twigs are ignored, even if they are collected from an adjoining branch on the limb from which the nymphs and eggs were taken. From the writer's fairly extended observations it would seem that seasonal abundance of certain fulgoroid species is occasioned fully as much by seasonal suitability of the sap of the host plant group— it is rare that only a single plant species is involved—as by a temporary scarcity of parasites, though the evidence in support of this supposition cannot be presented here. The nogodinid *Bladina fuscana* Stål attacks pineapple and the ornamental *Rhoeo discolor*, spending the day among the brown vegetable debris that collects at the leaf bases and becoming active toward dusk. The minor fulgoroid pests of Gramineae are too numerous to list; it is permissible to single out *Oliarus maidis* (described below), which is rather abundant on maize, living like other members of this cixiid genus below ground in the nymphal stage and feeding on roots, and to mention the extensive delphacid genus *Delphacodes*, species of which attack *Axonopus compressus*, the common lawn and pasture grass of Trinidad.

The following notes outline the characteristics of the two localities most frequently given in the descriptions:

Santa Margarita, Mount St. Benedict, Northern Range, Trinidad: A small narrow valley traversed by a seasonal stream. It is occupied for most of its length by peasant cultivations and by shrubby secondary growth, and in its upper reaches passes into a cacao plantation and the drier type of mountain forest.

St. John's Valley, Northern Range: A wide valley lying to the east of the foregoing almost entirely occupied by cacao and mountain forest. Most of the collecting here was done along tracks on the edge of the forest at about 400 feet.

Superfamily FULGOROIDEA

Family CIXIIDAE

1a. *Antennae situated before eyes, in deep cavities, or with laminate or ledge-like processes below.*

Subfamily BOTHRIOCERINAE

Tribe BOTHRIOCERINI

Genus BOTHRIOCERA Burmeister

Bothriocera BURMEISTER, Handbuch der Entomologie, vol. 2, pt. 1, p. 156, 1835.
(Genotype, *B. tinealis* Burmeister, *ibid.*)

Vertex short, lateral margins somewhat produced anteriorly. Antennae placed before eyes, in deep cavities. Pronotum short; mesonotum large, tricarinate; tegmina moderately broad, Sc and R with a common stalk subequal in length to basal cell; R 3-branched, M 5-branched. Ovipositor complete.

BOTHRIOCERA BICORNIS (Fabricius)

PLATE 7, FIGURE 1

Issus bicornis FABRICIUS, Systema rhyngotorum, p. 101, 1803.—STÅL, Hemiptera Fabriciana, p. 93, 1869.

Two female specimens taken by the writer at Santa Margarita, Trinidad, B. W. I. (Aug. 17 and 28, 1942), resting on leaves of *Heliconia bihai* and cacao approach in tegminal pattern and general facies very closely to *B. bicornis* (Fabricius), where in the absence of type comparison they are provisionally placed.

1b. *Antennae situated below eyes, not in cavities, and devoid of processes below.*

Subfamily CIXIINAE

2a. *Tegmina steeply tectiform; abdomen laterally compressed, devoid of processes on segments 3 and 4; pygofer not flattened, usually slightly tumid; ovipositor complete.*

Tribe PINTALIINI

Genus PINTALIA Ståll

Pintalia STÅL, Svenska Vet.-Akad. Handl., new ser., vol. 3, No. 6, p. 4, 1862.
(Genotype, *P. lateralis* Ståll, designated by Muir, Pan-Pacific Ent., vol. 1, p. 103, 1925.)

Vertex with two subparallel transverse carinae; mesonotum tricarinate; tegmina steeply tectiform, Sc and R with a common stalk; R 3-branched, M 5-branched, arising separately from basal cell. Pygofer laterally compressed, lateral margins near anal angle often produced, medioventral process present. Anal segment of male much longer than broad, sometimes deflexed beyond anus, with ventral margin produced. Genital styles usually long, narrow at base, broader near apex. Periandrium tubular, penis reflexed distally. Ovipositor complete; pygofer longer than wide, depressed along middle line.

Pintalia albolineata MUIR, Trans. Ent. Soc. London, vol. 82, p. 435, 1934.

Male: Length, 4.4 mm.; tegmen, 5.0 mm. Female: Length, 4.9 mm.; tegmen, 5.5 mm.

Width of vertex between basal angles twice the length in middle, 2.6 times the width at apex; base deeply roundly emarginate, the transverse carina nearer to apex than to base, apex in dorsal view shallowly emarginate on each side of middle line. Length of frons in middle 1.4 times the greatest width, width at apex slightly more than twice width at base; median ocellus distinct.

Head pallid testaceous, sides of labrum and clypeus, and genae behind level of antennae brown, a small oblique pale stripe on genae behind ocellus and between eye and antenna; a sharply defined piceous area above posterior two-thirds of eye, extending on to vertex as far as a line between the side of the transverse carina and the trisection of the basal margin. Pronotum pallid on disk, fuscous behind eyes, and mottled with fuscous between postocular carinae and posterior margin; mesonotum reddish brown, fuscous laterally, with three or four pallid spots in posterior half of each lateral area. Legs dark testaceous or pale fuscous, abdomen fuscous. Tegmina translucent, lightly clouded with fuscous; three small spots in costal cell fuscous; longitudinal veins posterior to stigma and all transverse veins overlain with a slightly darker fuscous band; the apical margin lightly colored, the area between the commissural margin, the posterior claval vein, and the apex of the clavus pale; veins concolorous with membrane or slightly darker. Wings hyaline, faintly clouded with fuscous, veins darker. Pygofer of female pale with a fuscous border anteriorly.

Anal segment of male tubular with postanal portion deflexed through 60°, with a bulbous prominence ventrally at base. Aedeagus tubular, on right side a short spine directed posteriorly and a round fleshy pad distad of it near attachment of recurved membranous portion; on left side two spines near this attachment, one directed upward, then forward and slightly downward, the other posterior to it directed obliquely forward and upward; apical membranous portion with a spine arising from right side directed forward, then curved below appendage to left side and bending slightly upward. Genital styles in side view expanding apically, then tapering to a blunt point, a triangular projection on inner face near base. Pygofer with lateral angles only slightly produced, forming a blunt lobe; medioventral process triangular, wider across its base than long.

Anal segment of female short, tubular, 1.5 times as long as wide. ovipositor complete, long and curved upward.

Described from five males and six females collected by the writer at Santa Margarita (Oct. 25, 1942, Feb. 17, Mar. 12, 1943) resting on low bushes. Material deposited in U. S. N. M. and B. M. N. H. A male and a female were assigned to this species by Mr. China, who indicated that it is allied to *P. delicata* Fowler.

PINTALIA STRAMINEA, new species

PLATE 7, FIGURES 11-16

Male: Length, 4.0 mm; tegmen, 5.0 mm.

Width of vertex between posterior angles 1.6 times length in middle, 2.1 times width at apex, base deeply roundly emarginate, the transverse carina about equidistant from base and apex; apex in dorsal view shallowly emarginate. Length of frons in middle 1.2 times the width, width at apex slightly more than twice width at base; median ocellus distinct.

Head pallid testaceous, a yellowish-brown band on each side of middle line of frons, lateral margins of frons narrowly fuscous; sides of labrum, posterior half of sides of clypeus, and posterior third of genae below antennae fuscous; antennae pale, minutely speckled with black. Pronotum pale; mesonotum pale, suffused with fuscous on basal third of disk and narrowly along posterior lateral margin; carinae and scutellum pale; on each side of middle line anteriorly a clearly defined pale fuscous **V** extending basad for one-third of length of disk. Legs pale yellow, protibiae and mesotibiae pale fuscous. Abdomen pallid ventrally, tergites pale fuscous, genitalia pale yellow. Tegmina hyaline, yellowish, faintly suffused fuscous, slightly darker near commissural margin beyond apex of clavus; the margin itself is very pale yellow.

Anal segment of male tubular, the postanal portion scarcely deflexed, directed downward at extreme tip. Pygofer with each lateral angle considerably produced into a fingerlike lobe; medioventral process triangular, narrower across the base than long. Aedeagus tubular, on right side a process bifurcating into two spines two-fifths from base of aedeagus; on left side a horizontal spine directed posteriorly near base, a second spine directed anteriorly and slightly upward near attachment of reflexed membranous portion; membranous portion tubular with a sinuate flange on its left side. Styles long, narrow, almost symmetrically rounded at apex.

Described from two males collected by the writer at Santa Margarita, Trinidad, B. W. I. (Mar. 12, 1943), resting on a low bush. Holotype is U. S. N. M. No. 56674. This species is well distinguished from the preceding by its color pattern and by the shape of the genitalia.

2b. *Tegmina not usually steeply tectiform; abdomen generally not laterally compressed, devoid of processes on segments 3 and 4; ovipositor incomplete, pygofer broad, posteriorly flattened.*

Tribe CIXIINI

3a. *Media arising from basal cell.*

Subtribe CIXIINA

Genus MNEMOSYNE Stål

Mnemosyne STÅL, Berliner Ent. Zeitschr., vol. 10, p. 391, 1866. (Genotype, *M. cubana* Stål, *ibid.*)

Mesonotum with median and lateral carinae straight and strongly developed, with a more feeble arcuate carina on each side of middle line. Tegmina with M_3 and M_4 forking close to Mf, M_r and M_2 forking at a greater distance from Mf.

MNEMOSYNE ARENAE, new species

PLATE 7, FIGURES 17–26

Male: Length, 6.3 mm.; tegmen, 6.7 mm.   Female: Length, 6.0 mm.; tegman, 7.8 mm.

Vertex hollowed out, width between basal angles equal to length in middle, 2.3 times width at apex, base roundly emarginate; transverse carina curved anteriorly in middle to touch apex; no median carina on vertex. Base of frons visible from above, its anterior border in dorsal view slightly convex; lateral areolets not present at apex of vertex. Frons almost flat, its lateral margins diverging to level of antennae, thence curving mesad somewhat angularly down to fronto-clypeal suture; width of frons 1.1 times length in middle, width at apex 2.8 times width at base; median ocellus represented by a scar; median carina present throughout on frons and clypeus, sides of both carinate; rostrum reaching almost to tip of abdomen. Pronotum with a median carina and a carina on each side following the outline of the posterior margin of the eyes and turning posteriorly between eye and tegula. Tegulae carinate. Mesonotum with five carinae. Hind tibiae with two spines. Tegmina with veins granulate, a row of granules in cells Sc, R_1, M_3, M_4, Cu_{1a}, and Cu_{1b}, each granule bearing a microtrichous seta.

Vertex, clypeus, and genae testaceous, frons and labrum fuscous, median carina and frontoclypeal suture pallid, rostrum testaceous with the apical joint fuscous. Pronotum testaceous, a fuscous band between eye and tegula, a fuscous spot at inner angle of lateral lobe near antenna on each side; mesonotum testaceous or rufous, clouded fuscous anteriorly and outside lateral carinae. Legs testaceous, profemora and mesofemora tinged rufous, tarsi and postfemora fuscous.   Abdomen testaceous, suffused reddish brown.   Tegmina transparent ivory yellow, two faint fuscous spots in costal cell, a spot adjoining stigma basally, a diffuse fuscous cloud between R and M extending faintly across to claval suture; an irregular pale fuscous band from stigma to apex of clavus along transverse veins, a second irregular band across middle of apical cells of R and M, distal portion of apical cells and apical margin pale fuscous.   Wings hyaline, faintly clouded fuscous, slightly darker near apical margin, veins fuscous.

Anal segment of male deflexed through 110° beyond anal opening, in side view expanded at apex.   Pygofer viewed laterally with an angular prominence, a small but distinct emargination below it, whence the margin is produced posteriorly into an obtuse angle; medioventral process almost quadrate, its posterior margin sinuate and culminating in a median point.   Aedeagus tubular, a sclerotized horizontal portion passing upward at tip into a membranous flagellum, which is beset dorsally with a row of thin prominent spines and curves obiquely downward and anteriorly to the left side; an elongated sinuate horizontal process arising near base of aedeagus on left side produced posteriorly in a broad spine for two-thirds length of aedeagus.   Genital styles stout, broad in side view, curved in basal half upward and forward through 120° and expanding in distal half into a broad plate truncate apically.

Anal segment of female tubular, 2.5 times as long as broad.   Ovipositor narrow, porrect, the sheath longer than the anal segment.

Described from one male and one female collected in Arena Forest, Trinidad, B. W. I., by Dr. A. M. Adamson (Apr. 13, 1938) and one male collected by the writer in forest, Los Bajos, Trinidad (Nov. 15, 1942).   Type, U.S.N.M. No. 56776.

Genus OLIARUS Stål

Oliarus STÅL, Berliner Ent. Zeitschr., vol. 6, p. 306, 1862. (Genotype, *O. walkeri* Stål, designated by Distant, Fauna of British India, Rhynchota, vol. 3, p. 256, 1906.)

Mesonotum with five carinae; frons with a percurrent median carina, vertex with an acutely angular or curved transverse carina which joins the middle portion of the apical transverse carina, forming an areolet apically on each side.   Fork of M_1 and M_2 in the tegmina nearer to Mf than is the fork of M_3 and M_4.

OLIARUS BIPERFORATUS, new species

PLATE 7, FIGURES 27–36

Male: Length, 7.3 mm,; tegmen, 6.7 mm.   Female: Length, 8.2 mm; tegmen, 9.5 mm.

Vertex hollowed out, width between basal angles equal to or only slightly less than length in middle, 1.6 times width at apex, subangularly emarginate at base; transverse carina rounded apically, apical carina almost obsolete, a quadrate cell in middle line between anterior and posterior transverse carinae; base of frons visible from above, its anterior border in dorsal view slightly convex; frons almost flat in middle, raised near sides to form broad flanges in which a clear fenestra is situated a short distance in from the margin at the level of the antennae on each side; lateral margins diverging from base to level of antennae, thence evenly curved inward to frontoclypeal suture; width of frons 1.2 times length in middle, width at apex twice width at base; median ocellus present; median carina forked at extreme base, percurrent on frons and clypeus; rostrum reaching to apex of abdomen. Pronotum short, carinate medially and with lateral carinae following the posterior margin of the eyes, posterior border acutely angularly emarginate; mesonotum with five carinae, the intermediate pair almost complete. Posttibiae with three spines.

Vertex testaceous, areolets fuscous in middle; frons pale testaceous, a fuscous band on each side of middle line, fenestrae hyaline; clypeus fuscous, almost piceous basally on each side of median carina; genae pallid yellow, antennae testaceous; rostrum fuscous, piceous at tip. Pronotum fuscous anteriorly, pallid yellow on disk and between postocular carinae and posterior margin; mesonotum fuscous, a piceous band along middle line and outside lateral carinae. Legs testaceous, femora reddish fuscous. Abdomen testaceous, a piceous band along middle line dorsally, two round dark spots near each lateral border; sternites pallid, fuscous near sides anteriorly; genitalia testaceous. Tegmina hyaline, ivory yellow; stigma pale yellowish brown, a narrow fuscous spot in cell posterior to it; transverse veins overlaid with fuscous patches; apical cells distally fuscous, that of Cu_{1b} being wholly infuscate; veins dark, sparsely and minutely granulate. Wings hyaline, suffused fuscous near apical margin, veins fuscous, minutely granulate.

Anal segment of male tubular, not greatly produced behind anal opening, ovate in dorsal view. Aedeagus complex, consisting of a sclerotized tube directed horizontally backward with a membranous flagellum attached apically, reflected forward to lie above and to the left of the sclerotized limb; a large thick spine near base of aedeagus on right side curved outward then inward; two small spines on left side arising close together on a slight ridge, one directed outward, the other curved angularly inward and slightly upward; a large thick spinose process arising at about same level, crossing from left side to right and projecting outward and upward above aedeagus on right side; membranous flagellum slightly bulbous at base with a small basal spine, thence expanding distally into an elongate hollow cone with the ventral lip produced into a point. Genital styles short, each consisting of a straight limb terminating in a flat plate, quadrate in side view, with the inner angle slightly falcate; a small triangular flange on the inner face of each style. Pygofer with lateral angles smooth, bluntly rounded; medioventral process acutely triangular.

Anal segment of female approximately triangular in dorsal view, almost as broad as abdomen, width at base 1.9 times length. Pygofer broad, flattened. Ovipositor directed horizontally.

Described from one male and two females collected by the writer at Verdant Vale, Trinidad, B. W. I., on cacao (June 1936). Holotype male and allotype female, U.S.N.M. No. 56777; one paratype in B.M.N.H. This species is distinguished from other Trinidad forms by its large size, as well as by the coloring and by the genitalia of both sexes.

OLIARUS OPALINUS, new species

PLATE 7, FIGURES 37–41

Female: Length, 3.3 mm.; tegmen, 4.2 mm.

Vertex hollowed out, median length distinctly exceeding width across base (1.2 to 1), areolets reaching back to behind middle of lateral margins, a small quadrate cell between them apically; median carina absent. Frons longer than wide (1.1 to 1), margins sinuately diverging to below level of antennae then curving inward to suture; median carina present on frons and clypeus; median ocellus present. Pronotum short, lateral carinae diverging to follow hind margin of eyes; mesonotum with intermediate carinae distinct in basal half, obsolete in apical half. Hind tibiae with four spines, the basal pair minute. Tegmina with Cu forking basad of Sc and R, stigma elongate, oblique, narrowly oval; veins sparsely and minutely granulate.

Vertex brownish testaceous, slightly darker near margins and inside areolets; frons clouded with fuscous, darkest near middle, median carina and lateral submarginal areas testaceous, lateral margins narrowly fuscous; clypeus testaceous, lightly clouded fuscous on disk, dark fuscous on sides and distally, excluding the median carina which is testaceous. Pronotum testaceous clouded with pale fuscous except near margins; mesonotum reddish brown. Legs testaceous. Abdominal tergites and sternites reddish brown, anal segment testaceous. Tegmina transparent, slightly yellowed; stigma rather pale, veins yellow. Wings vitreous.

Anal segment very much broader than long (2.4 to 1), broadly triangular.

Described from one female collected at Caracas, Venezuela, by Dr. J. G. Myers (Dec. 23, 1930). Type, U.S.N.M. No. 56675. This species differs from *O. maidis* (described below), in size, the shape of the vertex, and the color, and from other species treated in the present report in the shape of the anal segment.

OLIARUS QUADRATUS, new species

PLATE 7, FIGURES 42–44

Female: Length, 3.0 mm.; tegmen, 3.8 mm.

Vertex hollowed, median length markedly exceeding width across base (1.3 to 1), areolets reaching back to one-third from base of lateral margin, a small quadrate cell between them apically; median carina absent, a median notch present basally; greatest length of frons slightly exceeding greatest width (13 to 12), frons shallowly grooved near margins; median carina present, distinctly forked near base; median ocellus present; lateral margins diverging to below level of antennae then curving inward. Pronotum short, lateral carinae diverging to follow hind margin of eyes. Hind tibiae with four spines, the basal pair minute; hind tarsi very long, three-quarters as long as hind tibiae, the basi-tarsal joint about twice as long as second and third combined. Tegmina with M forking about level with apex of clavus, Cu forking basad of Sc and R; veins conspicuously granulate, each granule bearing a macrotrichous seta. Anal segment a little broader than long (1.2 to 1), almost quadrate.

Vertex, frons, genae, and antennae fuscous to piceous, margins testaceous, clypeus testaceous to fuscous, piceous near apex; rostrum testaceous, apical joint fuscous. Pronotum fuscous, margins testaceous; mesonotum and abdomen fuscous. Fore and middle legs pale fuscous, tibiae testaceous, tarsi dark, hind femora pale fuscous, tibiae and tarsi pale testaceous. Anal segment fuscous. Tegmina vitreous, stigma dark, rather broadly ovoid, veins yellow, clouded fuscous, granules clear, bordered fuscous, setae dark; a fuscous cloud across base of costal cell, basal cell, and along inner border of clavus; a fuscous spot at Sc fork, Cu_1 fork and on M between these two, and also on commissural margin near its juncture with the united claval veins; a fuscous cloud over all the transverse veins and over the tip of Cu_{1b}. Wings vitreous, veins pale fuscous.

Described from one female collected by Dr. Myers at Caracas, Venezuela (Dec. 23, 1930). Type, U.S.N.M. No. 56676. This species differs from the preceding in the shape of the vertex, in the forking of the median carina, the proportionate length of the hind tarsus, the color, and size.

OLIARUS MAIDIS, new species

PLATE 7, FIGURES 45–54

Male: Length, 3.0 mm.; tegmen, 3.5 mm. Female: Length, 3.0 mm.; tegmen, 4.5 mm.

Median length of vertex scarcely shorter than width across base; areolets reaching back to midpoint of lateral margins, a small quadrate cell between them medially at apex; median carina absent or scarcely indicated near notch at base. Frons with lateral margins sinuately diverging to level of antennae, thence curving inward to suture; greatest width 1.25 times median length; median carina percurrent on frons and clypeus, forked very near base. Pronotum with median carina and with lateral carinae following hind margin of eyes; mesonotum with five carinae, the intermediate carinae long and complete. Hind tibiae with two spines, one minute basally, the other at middle. Tegmina with Cu_1 forking distinctly basad of Sc and R.

Head piceous, a dull yellow spot at posterior end of areolets; median areolet, median carina and lateral margins of frons, outer portion of frontoclypeal suture and second joint of antennae dull yellow. Pronotum fuscous or piceous, lateral carinae and posterior margin dull yellow, mesonotum piceous; abdomen fuscous or piceous, membrane pallid. Femora piceous, protibiae and mesotibiae testaceous bordered fuscous, protarsi and mesotarsi fuscous, metatibiae and tarsi pale testaceous. Tegmina hyaline, a light mark at basal end of stigma, veins brown with sparse swollen tubercles. Wings hyaline, veins brown, granular.

Anal segment of male broadly ovoid in dorsal view, longer than broad (1.3 to 1). Aedeagus complex, apodeme of penis curving toward right posteriorly, a prominent finger-shaped tube lying obliquely from near posterior end of apodeme across to left side of aedeagus, a set of four spines near its posterior end, comprising two apical spines, of which one is curved almost in a circle and the other directed upward and backward, and two lateral spines directed forward. Periandrial membrane broad, shallowly curved, forming a broad lobe distally on right side.

Anal segment of female very broad in dorsal view, three times as broad as long, subtriangular in outline.

Described from 3 males and 11 females collected by the writer at St. Augustine, Trinidad, B. W. I., on maize (July 13, 14, 1942). Holotype and allotype, U.S.N.M. No. 56677; paratypes in B.M.N.H. This species is distinguished by the shape of the male genitalia and in the female by that of the anal segment.

3b. Media arising from a common stalk with Sc and R.

Subtribe MYNDINA

PARAMYNDUS, new genus

Vertex longer than broad, shallowly depressed in middle, more so near base, sides elevated, anterior margin very slightly convex, posterior margin very shallowly excavated, median carina present only at base. Frons longer than broad, slightly curved in side view, margins diverging to below level of antennae thence incurved to frontoclypeal suture; median carina distinct, median ocellus absent; a shallow depression inside and parallel to each lateral margin. Clypeus almost flat with median and lateral carinae present. Eyes slightly excavated ventrally; antennae with first joint ringlike, second joint globose. Pronotum narrow near middle, posterior border rather shallowly emarginate; median carina present, disk almost square, a curved oblique carina on each side from behind eye to posterior lateral angle, a straight carina on each side between eye and tegula; mesonotum with median and lateral carinae, the latter diverging slightly posteriorly; scutellum pointed. Hind tibiae without lateral spines but with six apical spines arranged in two groups of three. Tegmina rather long with costal and commissural margins almost parallel, apical margin almost symmetrically rounded. Stem $Sc+R+M$ long, half as long as stem $Sc+R$; Sc and R forking at apical third, M forking distinctly distad of Sc fork, Cu_1 forking slightly basad of fork of Sc and R, a conspicuous indentation in middle of Cu_{1a}; veins studded with sparse granules with a seta arising from each. Ovipositor complete.

Genotype: *Paramyndus cocois*, new species.

PARAMYNDUS COCOIS, new species

PLATE 8, FIGURES 55-63

Male: Length, 3.7 mm.; tegmen, 3.8 mm. Female: Length, 3.9 mm.; tegmen, 3.9 mm.

Vertex longer than broad (2.3 to 1), frons longer than broad (1.1 to 1).

Head and body uniformly pallid green in life, with anterior border of mesonotum narrowly fuscous or piceous beneath overlapping edge of pronotum; tergites of abdomen medially faintly clouded fuscous. Spines on legs black-tipped. Eyes purplish red.

Anal segment of male long, projecting just beyond aedeagus, tubular. Pygofer with lateral margins triangularly lobate; ventral margin straight, medioventral process tonguelike, curved downward apically, with a median vertical plate below. Aedeagus tubular, a long spine on left side near apex curved upward then horizontally and anteriorly, a second long spine on right side near apex directed obliquely downward and anteriorly; a sclerotized rod on left side below apex expanding abruptly into a rounded membranous plate adpressed to aedeagus. Genital styles with a narrow basal stalk, expanding abruptly near apex into an approximately ovate plate.

Anal segment of female tubular, short, about as long as telson.

Described from 15 males and 25 females taken by the writer at St. Augustine, Trinidad, B. W. I., on coconut leaves, sugarcane, and Guatemala grass on various dates in each month between July and November 1942. Holotype and allotype, U.S.N.M. No. 56678; paratype in B.M.N.H. This genus is apparently near *Haplaxius* Fowler, and according to Mr. China, who compared it with the type, differs in the absence of tubercles on the veins (the tubercles being very pronounced in *Haplaxius*), and in having the frons less broad, its margins less convex, and the vertex more parallel-sided than Fowler's genus.

Family DELPHACIDAE

4a. Calcar subulate or spiniform, without lateral teeth.

Subfamily ASIRACINAE

Genus PENTAGRAMMA Van Duzee

Pentagramma VAN DUZEE, Bull. Buffalo Soc. Nat. Sci., vol. 5, p. 260, 1897. (Genotype, *Liburnia vittatifrons* Uhler, Bull. U. S. Geol. and Georgr. Surv. Terr., vol. 2, p. 351, 1876; vol. 4, p. 510, 1878.)

Head about as broad as prothorax, vertex longer than broad, sides subparallel, anteriorly rounded; frons broadly ovate, devoid of median carina but with two intermediate carinae parallel to lateral margins; antennae rather long, smooth, narrow, II much longer than I. Pronotum with lateral carinae not reaching hind margin; mesonotum with five carinae. Pygofer long, styles directed posteriorly rather than vertically.

PENTAGRAMMA BIVITTATA Crawford

PLATE 8, FIGURES 64–67

Pentagramma bivittata CRAWFORD, Proc. U. S. Nat. Mus., vol. 46, p. 566, 1914.

Female: Length, 6.5 mm.; tegmen, 6.1 mm.

Frons and genae fuscous, a pale band passing below each eye and somewhat arcuately across basal third of frons; a second pale band across frons near frontoclypeal suture, continued below antennae. Antennae with second joint prismatic, both joints with a black longitudinal stripe anterodorsally. Clypeus fuscous, paler on sides, where there is a single dark spot distad of middle.

Anal segment of female short, tubular, in dorsal view not quite so broad as long: preceding abdominal segment in dorsal view narrow.

Ovipositor with numerous small, even, peglike teeth on dorsal border of first valvulae.

A single female collected on sugarcane in Trinidad, B. W. I., by D. Farrell (1920) is placed here.

Genus EUCANYRA Crawford

Eucanyra CRAWFORD, Proc. U. S. Nat. Mus., vol. 46, p. 568, 1914. (Genotype, *E. stigmata* Crawford, *ibid.*, p. 569.)

Vertex narrow, longer than wide, projecting beyond eyes; frons with a median carina narrowly forked toward base; antennae rather long, terete. Pronotum tricarinate; mesonotum quinquecarinate. Tegmina large, with a prominent stigma; a very distinct transverse vein from stigma to apex of clavus. Pygofer elongate; genital styles short. Anal segment asymmetrical.

EUCANYRA FLAGELLATA, new species

PLATE 8, FIGURES 68-74

Male: Length, 4.6 mm.; tegmen, 4.3 mm.

Vertex longer than broad, curving uninterruptedly on to frons, a transverse carina about level with middle of eye, a carina arising at each of its ends and converging anteriorly to form median frontal carina one-third from base of frons; frons longer than broad (2.3 to 1), lateral margins diverging to below level of antennae, thence slightly curved inward to suture; clypeus long, with median and lateral carinae; antennae cylindrical, long, the first joint smooth, the second 1.6 times longer than the first, beset with round sensory pits and setae. Pronotum short, tricarinate; mesonotum broad, quinquecarinate. Tegmina with fork of Sc and R basad of Cu_1 fork, a broad stigmatic area at anterior end of tranverse veins; veins setigerous. Legs long, hind tibiae with three spines before apex; posttibial spur quadrangular, spinose, slightly more than half as long as basitarsus.

Head testaceous, median carina of frons and clypeus with an indistinct fuscous band on each side, a small fuscous or piceous area on genae with four pale spots below base of antennae, rostrum testaceous. Pronotum and mesonotum pale fuscous. Legs testaceous, apex of femora, two bands on protibiae and mesotibiae, and protarsi and mesotarsi fuscous. Abdomen pale fuscous strongly tinged red. Tegmina hyaline, yellowish, veins broad, interruptedly marked fuscous; stigma pale fuscous; transverse veins hyaline, bordered fuscous; apical cells fuscous at margin. Wings hyaline, faintly clouded fuscous, veins brown.

Anal segment of male in dorsal view short, with sides expanding unequally to near apex; greatest width subequal to length; telson one-half as long as anal segment. Pygofer long, anal emargination wide and rather deep, lateral margins produced caudad to form a lobe shallowly indented at apex, and about two-thirds as long as genital styles; ventral hind margin sinuate, devoid of medioventral process. Aedeagus comprising a narrow tube with a very long tubular flagellar appendage at apex, this appendage being widely curved through a complete circle dorsad; a small flat pointed lobe on its inner margin halfway from base, a very long thin filament arising on inner margin toward apex, the flagellar appendage itself tapering to a short sharply deflexed point. Genital styles broad at base, slightly diverging to their midpoints, then angularly converging almost to meet at apex; outer margin with sides almost straight, angularly bent at middle, inner margin straight for one-quarter from base, then deeply concave, becoming slightly convex before apex, so that the two styles enclose a heart-shaped cavity; apex of each style rounded into a blunt point.

Described from one male specimen collected in Trinidad, B. W. I., by F. W. Urich (1920). This species differs from *stigmata* Crawford in size, in the shape of the genital styles, aedeagus, and anal segment, and in the color pattern. Holotype, U.S.N.M. No. 56679.

Genus TETRASTEIRA Muir

Tetrasteira MUIR, Bull. Hawaiian Sugar Planters' Exp. Stat., ent. ser., No. 18, pt. 1, p. 4, 1926. (Genotype, *T. minuta* Muir, *ibid.*)

Head narrower than pronotum; vertex wider than long, with a V-shaped transverse carina dividing frons from vertex; frons longer than broad, median carina simple; antennae terete, small. Pronotum with lateral carinae reaching hind margin, median carina feeble; mesonotum with four carinae, inner pair not reaching hind margin, outer pair attaining it. Legs comparatively short, tibial spur awl-shaped. Ovipositor complete.

TETRASTEIRA ALBITARSIS, new species

PLATE 8, FIGURES 75–84

Male: Length, 1.9 mm.; tegmen, 2.0 mm.

Vertex very short and wide, with a carina in the shape of a wide inverted V; frons 1.6 times longer than broad, widest in apical half. Pronotum with median carina strongly present, mesonotum with four carinae, both pairs distinctly reaching hind margin. Hind tibiae with two spines. Tegmina with a strong fold on costal margin at stigma. Wings emarginate at suture.

Dark brown, lighter over tegulae, base of tegmina, and a small triangular spot at costal fold; veins dark, except the cross veins at nodal line which are light; wings smoky, veins dark, tibiae at apex and tarsi pallid.

Anal segment small, short, very symmetrically produced posteriorly on each side into a small rounded deflexed lobe; lateral margins deeply sinuate, produced into a rounded lobe ventrally; ventral hind margin deeply excavated. Diaphragm short, without armature. Periandrium produced into a broad plate along right side with an outwardly directed point near apex; penis with apodeme traversing periandrium, with a curved spine directed ventrad at apex, and a curved membranous lobe, supported by a sclerotized rod, on left directed laterad. Genital styles narrow, outer margin straight, somewhat convex near apex, inner margin slightly convex at base, concave near apex. Apex rounded, somewhat bent mesad.

Described from one male taken by the writer in St. John's Valley, Trinidad, B. W. I. (June 12, 1942). This species differs from *minuta* Muir in size, in the carinae of the pronotum and mesonotum, in the anal segment, and in the genitalia. Type, U.S.N.M. No. 56680. It will be noted that the length of the inner pair of mesonotal carinae is variable, and does not constitute a character of generic value as originally believed.

4b. Calcar cultrate, thick, convex on each side or slightly concave on inner face, or thin and tectiform, toothed along hind margin, or without teeth.

Subfamily DELPHACINAE

5a. Calcar convex on each side, toothed on posterior margin.

Tribe ALOHINI

Genus BURNILIA Muir

Burnilia MUIR, Bull. Hawaiian Sugar Planters' Exp. Stat., ent. ser., No. 15, p. 7, 1924. (Genotype, *Delphax pictifrons* Stål, Ent. Zeit. Stettin, vol. 25, p. 50, 1864.)

Head narrower than thorax; vertex 1.5 times as long as wide across base, base 1.5 times width at apex, sides straight, carinae forming an inverted Y in apical half; frons twice as long as wide at apex, apex 2.7 times width of base, frons strongly depressed across middle; antennae terete, nearly reaching to apex of clypeus, length of segment I twice its width, II 2.4 times length of I; clypeus in side view produced angularly in middle, carinate medially and laterally. Pronotum tricarinate, lateral carinae reaching hind margin; mesonotum tricarinate, flat on disk. Hind basitarsus considerably longer than other two joints together; calcar narrow, cultrate, thick, convex on both sides with about nine spines on hind margin.

BURNILIA SPINIFERA, new species

PLATE 8, FIGURES 85, 86

Male: Length, 3.8 mm.; tegmen, 4.1 mm.

Length of vertex 1.4 times width at base, base not quite twice as wide as apex, sides straight, apex projecting slightly beyond eyes, base situated slightly behind middle of eyes; frons 1.7 times' longer than wide at apex, lateral margins almost straight on basal two-thirds, thence arcuately expanding to apex; concave in middle; median carina distinct except at apex; antennae not reaching to apex of clypeus, second segment three times as long as the first.

Stramineous, apex of vertex and basal third of frons very pale fuscous, a round fuscous spot above each eye; a white band across apical third of frons widely bordered fuscous basally, narrowly so distally; a white spot bordered with black near lateral margin of pronotum; second antennal segment fuscous dorsally and at apex; pro- and mesofemora with a very pale fuscous spot at apex, metafemora with a dark spot. Tegmina hyaline, yellowish, veins concolorous; wings-hyaline, veins stramineous.

Anal segment long, semitubular, anus at apex. Pygofer with anal angle produced about half the length of anal segment, somewhat flattened and roughened distally and curved mesad, rounded at apex; a broad short spine, directed outward, arising inside lateral margin below anal angle, ventrad of this a second more slender spine directed obliquely upward; medioventral process consisting of two straight slender spines joined near base. Diaphragm with a long slender spine dorsally on each side of middle. Penis very slender, cylindrical. Genital styles in side view broad with dorsal margin deeply concave, apex obliquely truncate; a stout triangular tooth on inner face of style at apex; outer margin of style sinuately convex.

Described from one male specimen collected at Mabaruma, Northwest District, British Guiana, by J. G. Myers (Feb. 1931). Type, U. S. N. M. No. 56681. This species differs from *pictifrons* Stål and *williamsi* Muir in the genitalia, and from both and the female types of *belemensis* Muir, *heliconiae* Muir, and *longicaput* Muir in the proportions of the head and antennae, and in color pattern.

5b. *Calcar thick or thin, concave on inner surface, devoid of teeth on hind margin.*

Tribe TROPIDOCEPHALINI

Genus MALAXA Melichar

Malaxa MELICHAR, Philippine Journ. Sci., vol. 9D, p. 275, 1914. (Genotype, *M. acutipennis* Melichar, *ibid.*)

Vertex longer than broad, wider at base than at apex, the inverted V-shaped carina nearly touching the apex. Frons long, narrow, gradually widened to apex, sides straight, median carina simple; clypeus tricarinate; genae wide; antennae reaching beyond apex of clypeus, cylindrical, second segment much longer than first. Hind basitarsus longer than other two joints together; calcar shorter than basitarsus, thick, slightly concave on inner surface, devoid of teeth on hind margin. Tegmina narrow, apex of clavus almost bisecting hind border.

MALAXA GRACILIS, new species

PLATE 8, FIGURES 87–94

Male: Length, 3.0 mm.; tegmen, 4.3 mm.

Head distinctly narrower than pronotum; vertex longer than broad (1.5 to 1), slightly hollowed out, anteriorly curving on to frons, apex slightly narrower than base, only slightly projecting before eyes; an inverted V-shaped carina anteriorly nearly reaching apex in middle; posterior border transverse; frons narrow, flattened, twice as long as wide at apex, apex almost three times as wide as base, median carina unforked, lateral margins very slightly concave, sutural line impressed; clypeus markedly tumid, slightly longer than frons, gradually tapering distally, tricarinate; antennae long, tubular, basal joint three-quarters length of frons, seven times as long as wide, second joint twice as long as first, 11 times as long as wide, beset with setae and on distal half with rather sparse sensorial pits, third joint and flagellum subequal to basal joint; eyes large, widely emarginate below. Pronotum short, posterior margin obtusely angularly excavated, lateral carinae not reaching posterior margin; mesonotum tricarinate, disk curved, scutellum flat. Legs long and slender; spur thick, crescentic, concave on inner surface, devoid of teeth on hind border. Tegmina long, narrow, produced well beyond apex of abdomen, expanding in width for three-quarters of length from base then tapering; fork of Sc and R slightly basad of apex of clavus, Cu_1 fork at basal third; Cu_{1b} forked near apex, remainder simple at apex. Wings scarcely three-quarters length of tegmina.

Head stramineous, base of clypeus with a piceous band, a fuscous transverse band near apex; second joint of antennae pale fuscous in basal third, piceous in apical third; eyes red. Pronotum stramineous, inner angle of lateral lobes broadly piceous; a fuscous band on pleurite before mesocoxae; mesonotum fuscous, stramineous at lateral angles, tegulae stramineous. Legs stramineous, femora darker dorsally. Abdominal sclerites dorsally fuscous, ventrally pallid, fuscous anterolaterally, flecked with an orange spot posterolaterally; genitalia fuscous.

Anal segment short, ringlike, sunk into anal emargination of pygofer, anal style very short, triangular. Pygofer with a deep anal emargination, anal angles produced into points and nearly meeting beneath anal segment, opening about as long as wide; a slender stalked bifurcate process medioventrally a little below lower margin of opening. Penis narrowly tubular basally, with a wide, pendent, laterally compressed semimembranous appendage, devoid of teeth, arising subapically and reflected anteriorly ventrad. Genital styles broad, especially at middle, directed upward and outward, basal angles strongly produced upward; outer margin concave near base, then strongly convex, becoming concave again before apex, inner margin concave basally, then convex, then sinuately tapering to pointed apex.

Described from a single male specimen collected at Caracas, Venezuela, by Dr. J. G. Myers (Dec. 6, 1930). Type, U.S.N.M. No. 56682. This species differs from *occidentalis* Muir in the shape of the genitalia, especially of the penis.

5c. Calcar thin, foliaceous or tectiform, with teeth along hind margin.

Tribe DELPHACINI

Genus SACCHAROSYDNE Kirkaldy

Saccharosydne KIRKALDY, Bull. Hawaiian Exp. Stat. Div. Ent. No. 3, p. 139, 1907. (Genotype, *Delphax saccharivora* Westwood, Mag. Nat. Hist., vol. 7, pp. 496, 610, 1834.)

Head angular in profile; vertex about twice as long as wide at base, projecting well beyond eyes, an inverted V-shaped carina present; frons about twice as long as wide; antennae short, reaching to base of clypeus; second segment of antenna twice the length of the first.

SACCHAROSYDNE SACCHARIVORA (Westwood)

PLATE 8, FIGURES 95–102

Delphax saccharivora WESTWOOD, Mag. Nat. Hist., vol. 7, pp. 496, 610, 1834.

Male: Length, 2.6 mm.; tegmen, 3.6 mm. Female: Length, 3.4 mm.; tegmen, 3.7 mm.

Light green during life; a narrow longitudinal black line anterodorsally on both segments of antennae.

Genital styles tapering distally, curved beyond middle and recurved near apex. Penis consisting of a horizontal, slightly curved plate directed posteriorly; below this a short stout spine, curving upward distally, and directed posteriorly; at base of this spine a long whiplike tapering filament, broad and sinuate near point of attachment, with a strongly refractive line in middle traversing the basal part.

Two males and two females collected by D. Farrell on sugarcane in Trinidad (July 31, 1920) and one female collected by the writer on the same host at Caroni, Trinidad, B. W. I. (May 5, 1936), are at hand. This species is distinguished from the other six of the genus by the proportions of the vertex and by the shape of the genitalia.

Genus PEREGRINUS Kirkaldy

Peregrinus KIRKALDY, Entomologist, vol. 37, p. 175, 1904. (Genotype, *Delphax maidis* Ashmead, Psyche, vol. 5, p. 323, 1890.)

Frons at least twice as long as wide; vertex not longer than broad, truncate or slightly rounded at apex, carinae of vertex distinct; antennae terete, not flattened, II considerably longer than I, I longer than broad. Head narrower than pronotum; lateral carina of pronotum straight, diverging, reaching hind margin or near it.

PEREGRINUS MAIDIS (Ashmead)

Delphax maidis ASHMEAD, Psyche, vol. 5, p. 323, 1890.

Twenty-three males and 28 females collected by the writer on maize at St. Augustine, Trinidad, B. W. I. (May 3, 1942), were typical. Representative material in U.S.N.M.

Genus SOGATA Distant

Sogata DISTANT, Fauna of British India, Rhynchota, vol. 3, p. 471, 1906. (Genotype, *S. dohertyi* Distant, *ibid.*, p. 471, fig. 258.)

Body narrow and slender, head approximately as wide as pronotum; vertex truncate or slightly rounded at apex, not wider than eye on same level at base; carinae of vertex and frons distinct; frons longer than broad; antennae terete, with II longer than I, I longer than broad. Pronotum with lateral carinae reaching hind margin, not in line with mesonotal carinae.

SOGATA FURCIFERA (Horváth)

PLATE 9, FIGURES 116, 117

Delphax furcifer HORVÁTH, Termés. Füzetek, vol. 22, p. 372, 1899.

One macropterous male collected at St. Augustine, Trinidad, B. W. I., by the writer (May 3, 1942) on *Axonopus compressus*.

Genus DELPHACODES Fieber

Delphacodes FIEBER, Verh. zool.-bot. Ges. Wien, vol. 16, p. 524, pl. 8, fig. 32, 1866. (Genotype, *D. mulsanti* Fiéber, *ibid.*)

Head almost as broad as pronotum; vertex not longer than broad, or scarcely so, truncate or slightly rounded at apex; frons narrow, much longer than broad, carinae distinct, the median carina forked at base; antennae terete, rounded, first segment short, as broad as long.

Tegmina and wings normal (macropterous forms) or reduced (brachypterous forms). Posttibial spur thin, tectiform, minutely toothed on hind margin.

DELPHACODES TEAPAE (Fowler)

PLATE 9, FIGURE 115

Liburnia teapae FOWLER, Biologia Centrali-Americana, Rhynch.: Hom., vol. 1, p. 135, 1905.

One macropterous male was collected by the writer on *Axonopus compressus* at St. Augustine, Trinidad, B. W. I. (May 3, 1942).

DELPHACODES PROPINQUA (Fieber)

Delphax propinqua FIEBER, Verh. zool.-bot. Ges. Wien, vol. 16, p. 525, pl. 8, fig. 24, 1866.

Eight males (7 macropterous and 1 brachypterous) and four brachypterous females collected by Dr. E. McC. Callan at St. Augustine, Trinidad, B. W. I., are at hand. The detailed structure of the genital styles and penis agrees entirely with Muir's figures of a Puerto Rican specimen.

DELPHACODES PALLIDIVITTA, new species

PLATE 9, FIGURES 103–106

Male: Length 1.9 mm.; tegmen, 2.1 mm.

Width of vertex subequal to length, or very slightly greater, base wider than apex, situated just behind middle of eyes; frons viewed anteroventrally twice as long as broad, sides very slightly arcuate; second segment of antennae scarcely twice length of first, first distinctly longer than wide. Pronotum with lateral carinae divergent, slightly curved, not reaching hind margin. Hind basitarsus subequal to second and third joints together, posttibial spur about two-thirds as long as basitarsus, thin, tectiform, with teeth on hind margin.

Fuscous, middle line of clypeus and frons, vertex, disk of pronotum and mesonotum, posterior half of genae, lateral lobes of pronotum, tegulae, and abdominal membrane white; clypeus, lateral carinae of frons and pronotum, antennae, a row of four round spots on genae below antennae, rostrum, and legs testaceous or stramineous, apart from a round spot on metacoxae; tegmina hyaline, faintly yellowish, veins yellow, a faint curved fuscous band across fourth to seventh apical cells submarginally, and overlying transverse veins at their bases, apex of claval veins fuscous. Wings hyaline, veins fuscous.

Opening of pygofer slightly longer than wide, anal emargination large, anal angles not produced, lateral margins entire, almost straight. Anal segment comparatively small with a pair of short slender spines on apical margin near middle directed ventrad. Penis tubular, narrowing apically, slightly sinuate and slightly laterally compressed, orifice on left side at apex, an oblique row of five spines above orifice, an oblique row of five spines on right side near middle, an oblique row of eight spines on left side arising dorsally in apical quarter and ending ventrally at basal quarter. Diaphragm with a narrow V-shaped process, minutely irregularly denticulate, situated medially below penis. Genital styles broad, outer margin sinuately curved, distally convex, inner margin convex in basal half, strongly concave in apical half, outer margin bent mesad distally to meet inner margin at apex.

Described from 25 macropterous males and 38 macropterous females collected by the writer on *Axonopus compressus* at St. Augustine, Trinidad, B. W. I. (Sept. 12, 1942). Holotype male and allotype female, U.S.N.M. No. 56683.

DELPHACODES AXONOPI, new species

PLATE 9, FIGURES 107–110

Male (macropterous): Length, 1.8 mm.; tegmen, 2.4 mm. Female (macropterous): Length, 2.1 mm.; tegmen, 2.9 mm.

Vertex as broad as long, or a very little shorter, base at middle of eyes, base as wide as apex; frons twice as long as wide, margins very slightly arcuate; antennae reaching slightly beyond base of clypeus, first segment longer than wide, second segment not quite twice as long as first. Posttibial spur three-quarters as long as basitarsus, thin, tectiform, with about 16 fine teeth.

Frons and clypeus black between yellow carinae, anterior portion of genae, apart from a few pale spots, basal joint of antennae, mesonotum, pleurites, abdominal sclerites, and genitalia fuscous, posterior half of genae, second joint of antennae, vertex, pronotum, and legs testaceous to light brown; tegmina hyaline, yellowish, veins dark yellow, sparsely granulate; wings vitreous, veins testaceous.

Opening of pygofer slightly wider than long, rounded, margins entire, anal emargination large, anal angles rounded, produced and curved mesad; diaphragm with dorsal margin sinuate, indented shallowly in middle. Anal segment comparatively small, sunk deeply into emargination, with a pair of slender spines apically, approximated at point of origin and directed downward. Penis subcylindrical, slightly compressed laterally, rounded at apex with orifice on left side; a row of 14 spines on left side arising dorsally near margin of orifice and passing downward to near ventral margin where six of the spines form a horizontal ledge; a horizontal row of six or seven spines ventrolaterally on right side. Genital styles flat, broad at base, narrower distally, apex produced into two short projections, the inner more slender, the margin between them shallowly convex toward its outer end, rather more markedly concave near inner projection, outer margin of style very slightly sinuate, inner margin with a slight projection beyond middle making the outline two unequal shallow concavities.

Female similar in color to male.

Described from one macropterous male and one macropterous female taken by the writer at St. Augustine, Trinidad, B. W. I. (July 18, 1942), on *Axonopus compressus*. Type male and allotype female, U.S.N.M. No. 56684. This species appears to be near *nigra* (Crawford), but differs in the aedeagus, having the orifice on the left side and a distinctly greater number of spines, as well as in the shape of the diaphragm and in the color of the antennae.

DELPHACODES SPINIGERA, new species

PLATE 9, FIGURES 111–114

Male (macropterous) : Length, 2.4 mm.; tegmen, 3.0 mm.

Width of vertex across base subequal to length or very slightly greater, base wider than apex, situated at middle of eyes; frons twice as long as wide, margins slightly arcuate; second segment of antennae scarcely twice length of first, first distinctly longer than wide. Pronotum with lateral carinae diverging, curved, not reaching hind margin. Hind basitarsus subequal to other two joints together; post-tibial spur two-thirds as long as basitarsus, thin, tectiform, toothed on hind margin.

Stramineous, a narrow sinuate band on each side of middle line of frons and clypeus, a horizontal band near lower edge of lateral lobes of pronotum, a spot on pronotum between eye and tegula, and a narrow line ȯn inner margin of tegulae fuscous; median carina of frons at basal fork, middle of vertex, pronotum and mesonotum pallid, bordered laterally tawny yellow on pronotum and mesonotum; tegmina hyaline, yellowish, veins concolorous, six apical veins with a small fuscous spot at margin; wings hyaline, veins darker.

Opening of pygofer about as long as wide, anal emargination large, anal angles not produced, lateral margins entire, very slightly curved, a minute point on each side level with ventral margin of diaphragm, a short setigerous toothlike process on posterior margin medioventrally. Anal segment comparatively small, with a single stout median spine directed ventrad on apical margin. Penis compressed laterally, deflexed obliquely, lower margin almost straight, dorsal margin curved downward apically and tapering to join lower in a slender point, much broader than lower margin, so that penis is narrowly V-shaped in cross section; diaphragm rather narrow, with armature absent or inconspicuous. Genital styles narrow, rounded, with an asymmetrical knob at apex, outer margin arcuate, inner margin correspondingly concave, basal angles obtuse, not prominent.

Described from a single macropterous male taken by the writer on *Axonopus compressus* at St. Augustine, Trinidad, B. W. I. (May 15, 1942.).   Type, U.S.N.M. No. 56685.

Family DERBIDAE

Tegmina relatively large, wings usually not less than half as long as tegmina, venation not greatly reduced.

Subfamily DERBINAE

6a. Clavus closed, sometimes narrowly open; common stalk of united claval veins not extending beyond apex of clavus; anterior sector of Cu₁ with not less than three veins.

Tribe DERBINI

Genus DERBE Fabricius

Derbe FABRICIUS, Systema rhyngotorum, p. 80, 1803.   (Genotype, *D. haemorrhoidalis* Fabricius, designated by Westwood, Proc. Linn. Soc. London, 1840, vol. 1, p. 83.)

Head narrow; antennae with first segment short, second segment large, subcylindrical, truncate at apex, densely studded with sensorial pits; tegmina large, veins prominent, media with anterior sector with five apical branches, posterior sector with six to eight apical branches; a short row of wax-bearing prominences developed on Sc and R, M, and Cu₁ basad of apex of clavus.

DERBE ULIGINOSA, new species

PLATE 9, FIGURES 118–123

Female: Length, 6.8 mm.; tegmen, 14.5 mm.

Tegmen with posterior sector of M with eight branches reaching margin, the cells posterior to the fourth to eighth of these branches each nine times as long as wide.

Fuscous, clypeus darker; posterior half of pronotum pallid, mesonotum with a large piceous spot on each side basally, legs testaceous, abdomen dorsally fuscous with a row of testaceous spots on each side of middle line, ventrally testaceous, genitalia fuscous; tegmina hyaline, ivory yellow, veins dark fuscous, a fuscous stripe along middle of cells basad of apex of clavus or anterior to posterior sector of media, a fuscous patch at commissural margin at end of oblique line of transverse veins; wings hyaline, a narrow fuscous stripe along middle of basal cells of R and M, apical margin clouded fuscous anteriorly, veins fuscous.

Anal segment obliquely deflexed, produced below anal opening into a quadrate plate with lateral angles produced, a pair of sclerotized sinuate rodlike processes arising near middle of hind margin directed posteriorly. Ovipositor with lateral styles moderately broad, tapering distally to a blunt point, not attaining tip of processes of anal segment, first valvulae with five or six oblique spines on dorsal margin distally. Subgenital plate in ventral view with hind margin curved backward into a broad median plate, approximately hexagonal in outline, with a narrow triangular process directed caudad arising on hind margin at middle.

Described from three female specimens collected in Trinidad, B. W. I., as follows: F. W. Urich, two specimens, one accompanied with a locality label "Maraval" (1916); D. Farrell, one specimen (1920). These specimens were taken by the writer from the collection of the former Imperial Department of Agriculture. This species is distinguished by the proportions of the apical cells of M in the tegmina, by the shape of the posterior border of the subgenital plate, and by the color pattern of tegmina and wings. Type, U.S.N.M. No. 56686.

DERBE BOLETOPHILA, new species

PLATE 9, FIGURES 124–128

Male: Length, 6.3 mm.; tegmen, 13.0 mm.

Tegmina with posterior sector of M with six branches reaching margin, the cells posterior to the third to sixth of these branches ten times as long as wide.

Head, thorax, legs, and genitalia pale stramineous; posterior half of pronotum, metanotum, and abdomen pallid, almost white; abdominal sclerites narrowly bordered red; tegmina and wings vitreous, anterior margin of tegmina narrowly lined red. Insect in life is very pale.

Anal segment long, rather flattened dorsoventrally, folded and deflexed at tip. Pygofer with lateral margins sinuate, ventral margin straight, medioventral process in form of a small lobe not quite semicircular. Aedeagus a simple sclerotized tube in basal portion; reflected apical portion viewed from left side trapezoidal with a membranous tube attached apically; three spines on left side of reflected limb, one anteroventrally near attachment, two near distal part of line of attachment, one spine long, decurved at tip, the other straight, two-thirds as long as preceding; on right side of aedeagus a long spine basad of reflected part directed obliquely upward, laterad of reflected part a broad lamina narrowing to a twisted bladelike process directed anteriorly, two spines of equal length on dorsal side of reflected part near its point of attachment. Genital styles narrow at base, widening to just beyond middle then narrowing to a point at apex, this being directed mesad; a complex cuplike fold projecting above dorsal margin at middle.

Described from a single male specimen taken by the writer in Caura Valley, Northern Range, Trinidad, B. W. I. (April 5, 1941), in forest, resting on fungus. Type, U.S.N.M. No. 56687. This species is well distinguished by the proportions of the apical cells of M in the tegmina, by the structure of the genitalia, and by the very pale color.

DERBE SEMIFUSCA, new species

PLATE 9, FIGURES 129–135

Male: Length, 6.5 mm.; tegmen, 15.0 mm.

Vertex short, subquadrate, somewhat produced before eyes; frons longer than broad (2.5 to 1), lateral margins slightly diverging distally, median carina absent; frontoclypeal suture deeply impressed; clypeus tricarinate, median carina obsolete at base; antennae with second segment subcylindrical, slightly expanding toward apex, terminal joint inserted apically on second. Pronotum short in middle, longer laterally anterior margin straight, posterior deeply emarginate; mesonotum inflated, upturned at scutellum. Tegmina with posterior sector of M with seven branches reaching margin, the cells posterior to the fifth, sixth, and seventh of these branches each six times as long as wide.

Head and body fuscous, clypeus at apex and on sides and mesonotum very dark, pronotum abruptly testaceous in posterior half, tegulae pale, abdomen dark testaceous dorsally, paler ventrally; tegmina with veins fuscous, all, with the exception of the apical veins of M and Cu_1, bordered with a broad hyaline band, middle portion of cells fuscous, apical cells of R and M_1 hyaline, a small dark patch on each of the apical branches of these veins near margin, remainder of apical cells fuscous; wings fuscous, veins fuscous bordered hyaline except near apical margin.

Pygofer with lateral margin sinuate, medioventral process large, nearly two-thirds as long as ventral posterior plate of pygofer, narrowly triangular, rounded at apex. Aedeagus in dorsal view subovate with three spinose processes arising two-thirds from base near left side, directed anteriorly, a long curved spine arising at same level and crossing obliquely forward to project beyond right margin, a broad lamina arising apically, directed forward and narrowing to a ribbonlike blade directed obliquely upward; at the basal end of this lamina a flattened spine directed anteriorly. Genital styles long, narrow, incurved at apex in a pincerlike manner, dorsal margin sinuate, a complex cuplike fold on dorsal margin at basal third.

Described from one male collected by F. W. Urich, Trinidad, B. W. I. (1916), taken from the collection of the former Imperial Department of Agriculture. Type, U.S.N.M. No. 56688, devoid of one tegmen, fore and middle tibiae and tarsi, and anal segment. This species is distinguished by its heavily infuscated tegmina and by the genitalia.

Genus MYSIDIA Westwood

Mysidia WESTWOOD, Proc. Linn. Soc. London, vol. 1, p. 83, 1840. (Genotype, *Derbe pallida* Fabricius, designated by Kirkaldy, Entomologist, vol. 36, p. 216, 1903.)

Vertex rather broad, short, lateral margins converging anteriorly; antennae cylindrical, expanding apically, heavily beset with sensory pits, a prominent notch on dorsal side at apex, in which terminal joint is inserted, arising therefore subapically; shoulder keels on pronotum absent or small; tegmina with M with three sectors, and with six or seven branches at margin, not even and parallel, Cu_1 with three sectors, the second forked before margin. Medium sized, usually pale colored, with a habit of carrying the tegmina and wings divergently upraised when at rest.

MYSIDIA CINEREA, new species

PLATE 9, FIGURES 136–150

Male: Length, 3.2 mm.; tegmen, 5.7 mm. Female: Length, 3.6 mm.; tegmen, 7.6 mm.

Vertex narrow in dorsal view, produced beyond eyes, about 1.1 times longer in middle than wide at base, 1.4 times wider across base than at apex, lateral margins slightly converging anteriorly, prominent; frons narrow, lateral margins gradually converging to below eyes then smoothly diverging to suture; clypeus about as long as frons, tricarinate; antennae with second joint longer than broad, slightly compressed laterally, strongly excavated at dorsal insertion of apical joint, beset with large sensoria. Pronotum short, anterior margin transverse, posterior margin angularly excavated, lateral lobes rather large; tegulae large; mesonotum broad, somewhat inflated, median carina obsolete. Tegmen with 8 to 12 pustules near base of $Sc+R$, three pustules near base of M.

Head, thorax, legs, and abdomen pallid, eyes red; tegmina hyaline, all veins faintly and broadly overlain with brown, a clear ellipsoidal spot near apical fork of M_1, with the vein tinged brown at fork, veins otherwise concolorous; wings hyaline, veins irregularly pale brown, apical cells clouded near margin, veins concolorous. Insect in life powdered pearly gray.

Anal segment of male short in dorsal view, produced distally below anal opening into a subquadrate plate, bearing an elongated process at each posterior angle. Pygofer with posterior margin sinuate, sloping obliquely forward at sides, medioventral process absent or represented by a slight sinuate dilation of the hind margin. Aedeagus a simple tube, a minute very broadly triangular spine on each side ventrally distad of middle, on dorsal surface a V-shaped groove above apex deepening distad to its midpoint. Genital styles broad, expanding distally, posterior margin in side view rounded, a small scroll-like process on dorsal margin near base.

Anal segment of female short, deflexed, bluntly triangular below anal opening. Lateral styles broad, bluntly rounded at apex, slightly longer than anal segment; first valvulae narrowed to a single apical spine curving upward at tip, two or three minute teeth subapically on dorsal margin. Medioventral process of subgenital plate in ventral view somewhat triangular, but bluntly rounded at apex.

Egg ellipsoidal, pointed at each pole, with three equidistant longitudinal carinae; pale, smooth, 0.5 mm. long, 0.3 mm. broad.

Described from two males and two females collected by the writer in St. John's Valley, Trinidad, B. W. I. (June 12, Sept. 13, 1942), resting on leaves in thick undergrowth. Holotype male and allotype, U.S.N.M. No. 56689; paratype in B.M.N.H.

6b. *Clavus and common stalk of united claval veins as above; anterior sector of Cu₁ with less than three veins, not joining media.*

Tribe CENCHREINI

OMOLICNA, new genus

Vertex broad, depressed along middle, lateral margins converging apically, apical margin straight or slightly concave, posterior margin shallowly excavated, width across base greater than length down middle, two rows of sensoria on raised area near each lateral margin; frons longer than wide at apex (about 2 to 1), width at apex approximately one and one-half times width at base, lateral margins diverging gradually to apex, devoid of granules, median carina absent, usually a longitudinal depression down middle of frons, a series of sensory pits inside each lateral margin; frontoclypeal suture impressed, clypeus slightly tumid with a median carina; genae devoid of a subantennal process. Pronotum with antennal foveae large. Tegmina long, parallel sided, $Sc+R+M$ fork at basal quarter, $Sc+R$ fork between basal third and middle of costal margin, subcostal cell long, M forking about level with apex of clavus, Cu_1 forking level or slightly distad of junction of claval veins, M with five veins reaching apical margin, three arising from a discal cell. Wings with R and M simple to apex, linked by a transverse vein four-fifths from base, Cu_{1a} forked just basad of its midpoint, where it is joined by a transverse vein from M, the limbs of the fork scarcely diverging to margin, Cu$_{1b}$ simple to apex, Cu$_2$ simple. Anal segment of male narrow, tubular, pygofer with a simple pointed medioventral process, genital styles incurved at apex. Anal segment of female very short, pregenital sternite with a broad lobe at middle of posterior margin. Egg bluntly ovoid, smooth, transparent, twice as long as broad.

Genotype: *Omolicna proxima*, new species.

This genus differs from *Syntames* Fowler in the absence of a median carina on the frons, from *Cenchrea* Westwood in the lower lateral carinae of the vertex and the tegminal and wing venation, and from *Phaciocephalus* Kirkaldy in tegminal and wing venation.

OMOLICNA PROXIMA, new species

PLATE 9, FIGURES 151–157; PLATE 10, FIGURES 158–160

Male: Length, 3.1 mm.; tegmen, 3.5 mm.   Female: Length, 3.1 mm.; tegmen, 3.6 mm.

Vertex wider between basal angles than long in middle (1.6 to 1), apical margin straight, basal margin obtusely excavated, 12 prominent sensory pits inside each lateral margin; frons twice as long as wide at apex, width at apex 1.8 times width at base, lateral margins diverging gradually to apex, lateral margins of vertex and frons not granulate, median carina absent, a longitudinal depression down middle of frons, a series of about 25 sensory pits inside each lateral margin; frontoclypeal suture impressed, clypeus slightly tumid with a median carina; no subantennal process present. Pronotum with antennal foveae large. Tegmina with Sc+R forking at basal two-fifths, M with five branches at apex, apical margin of tegmina minutely serrate, Sc+R and anterior claval vein with large pustules.

Vertex, clypeus, genae, rostrum, pronotum, and legs pale testaceous or pallid; frons, mesonotum, pleural and abdominal sclerites, and genitalia fuscous; tegmina pale fuscous, darker distad of stigma, veins pallid, margin hyaline to stigma, clear red around apex; wings hyaline, clouded fuscous, veins darker.

Anal segment of male long, tubular, deflexed through 40° beyond anal opening and angularly bent before tip to point almost vertically downward, a small lobe laterally midway along ventral margin. Pygofer with posterior margin almost straight laterally curving caudad ventrally, medioventral process broad, lobate at apex, produced laterally at middle of lateral margins, which are concave basally. Aedeagus tubular, two stout spines on right side, arising at base of flexible portion of aedeagus and directed anteriorly, slightly curved, three slender spines on left side; flexible portion medial, though arising from left side, shallowly hoodlike, sclerotized apically into a slender spine. Genital styles broad, abruptly rounded at apex and tapering to an incurved point; a pointed process on dorsal margin toward base, a small bifurcate process on ventral margin one-fifth from base.

Anal segment of female very short, postanal portion minute, lateral styles broad, parallel-sided, symmetrically rounded at apex. Ovipositor with first valvulae with two long spines apically, upturned at tip, above these an uncinate process bearing dorsally two or three minute spines and two larger spines apically. Medioventral portion of pregenital sternite somewhat longer than broad, posteriorly smoothly rounded. Egg 0.45 by 0.23 mm.

Described from 11 males and 9 females taken by the writer in St. John's Valley, Trinidad, B. W. I. (Sept. 21, 1942), resting on foliage. Holotype male and allotype, U.S.N.M. No. 56778; paratypes in B.M.N.H.

OMOLICNA RUBRIMARGINATA, new species

PLATE 10, FIGURES 161–168

Male: Length, 4.0 mm.; tegmen, 4.7 mm. Female: Length, 4.2 mm.; tegmen, 5.3 mm.

Width of vertex across base greater than length along middle (1.8 to 1), vertex curving into frons apically, not clearly separated from it, posterior border very obtusely emarginate; three rows of sensoria on each side of middle line, the outer pair on each side with larger sensoria than the inner row; frons longer than wide at apex (1.8 to 1), 1.4 times as wide at apex as at base, lateral margins expanding gradually to apex, median carina absent, middle of frons not much depressed, a series of about 30 sensory pits inside each lateral margin, which is slightly raised; frontoclypeal suture impressed; clypeus somewhat tumid with a distinct median carina; no subantennal process. Pronotum with antennal foveae large. Tegmina with Sc+R forking at basal two-fifths, M with five veins at apical margin, apical margin minutely serrate, Sc+R and anterior claval vein with large pustules.

Head, thorax, and abdominal sclerites testaceous, faintly suffused fuscous; rostrum and legs pale stramineous; tegmina transparent, yellow, slightly suffused fuscous, especially near stigma; apical margin and sometimes distal portion of apical veins pink, veins otherwise concolorous; wings hyaline, faintly clouded fuscous, veins darker.

Anal segment of male long, tubular, deflexed through 40° beyond anal opening and bent before apex to point downward, no lobe in middle of ventrolateral margin, but a slight flange before apex. Pygofer with lateral margins broadly sinuate, curved backward ventrally into a long tapering median process rounded at apex, keellike in lateral view and subequal in length to the pygofer. Aedeagus tubular, a pair of slender spines on dorsolateral margin about two-thirds from base, a large median membranous tube reflected to point anteriorly, with a pair of spines above and a pair below it, projecting somewhat beyond its tip, a pair of slender filaments two-thirds as long as aedeagus arising at point where it is recurved and directed anteriorly above the whole structure. Genital styles broad, expanding from base to middle, then narrowing to an inwardly directed point at apex; a small lobe between two notches on dorsal border about one-third from base.

Anal segment of female very short, postanal portion minute. Lateral styles broad, almost parallel-sided, symmetrically and bluntly rounded at apex. Ovipositor with first valvulae with two long spines apically, upturned at tip; above these an uncinate process bearing dorsally four curved spines near apex. Medioventral process of pregenital sternite almost semicircular.

Described from one male and two females collected by the writer in St. John's Valley, Trinidad, B. W. I. (Oct. 8, 1942), resting on low herbage. This species is distinguished by its size, by the shape of the frons and vertex, and by the arrangement of the sensoria on the vertex, by the shape of the anal segment, by the structure of the male genitalia, or in the female by the shape of the hind margin of the pregenital sternite, and by the color. Holotype male and allotype, U.S.N.M. No. 56690; paratype in B.M.N.H.

Genus NEOCENCHREA Metcalf

Neocenchrea METCALF, Journ. Elisha Mitchell Sci. Soc., vol. 38, p. 193, 1923.
(Genotype, *Cenchrea heidemanni* Ball, Can. Ent., vol. 34, p. 261, 1902.)

Vertex rather narrow, lateral margins raised, converging anteriorly; frons narrow, devoid of median carina, margins raised. Pronotum with deep antennal foveae. Tegmina elongate, narrow; Sc+R forking before level of apex of clavus, M forking just beyond apex of clavus, Cu₁ forking at level of junction of claval veins. Egg ovoid, smooth, transparent.

NEOCENCHREA GREGARIA, new species

PLATE 10, FIGURES 169–181

Male: Length, 4.5 mm.; tegmen, 5.4 mm. Female: Length, 5.0 mm.; tegmen, 5.9 mm.

Vertex as wide across base as long in middle, apex straight, minutely notched medially, hind border emarginate in a right angle; frons three times as long as wide in widest part, apex 1.2 times as wide as base, lateral margins almost straight, slightly widened at level of antennae, median carina absent; lateral margins of frons and vertex granulate; genae devoid of a subantennal process. Pronotum with antennal foveae large. Tegmina with Sc+R forking about middle, M forking at level of apex of clavus, with four veins reaching apical margin, Cu₁ forking level with junction of claval veins; anteroapical margin of tegmen minutely serrate.

Pale yellow, in life powdered a whitish fawn; lateral margins of vertex and frons, apical joint of rostrum, middle portion of abdominal tergites and genitalia fuscous; tegmina subopaque, powdered a very pallid fawn, veins concolorous; wings hyaline.

Anal segment of male long, tubular, deflexed through 40° beyond anal opening, bent before apex to point downward. Pygofer with sides slightly curved, ventrally curving backward to medioventral process, process subtriangular, truncate at apex and minutely notched medially. Aedeagus with a tubular sclerotized basal portion and an eversible apical lobe, the former with two spinose processes adpressed on right side at base, one process curved backward, downward, then upward, the other curved backward and upward, and bifurcate in a pincerlike manner apically; the flexible lobe complex and symmetrical, three spinose processes directed backward, arising near its base on each side, and above them a spinose process, slightly swollen in middle, directed obliquely upward and backward, a pair of large, somewhat bladelike, processes directed posteriorly, each swollen before apex, then narrowing to a deflexed sinuate filament; between these ventrally a pair of simple spinose processes directed posteriorly, curved upward distally. Genital styles in side view sinuately tapering to apex, a broad rounded flange projecting dorsally one-third from base, emarginate in middle of its upper edge, a minute outwardly directed tooth basad of the emargination, a digitate process, adpressed to side, arising near margin just distad of it.

Anal segment of female short, in side view with postanal portion deflexed through 60°. Lateral styles broad, curved inward, with dorsal and ventral apical angles shortly produced and bent mesad. First valvulae with four or five teeth on dorsal limb, two spinose processes at apex of ventral limb. Posterior border of pregenital plate almost semicircular. Egg ovoid, smooth, transparent, 0.45 by 0.26 mm.

Described from 15 males and 21 females taken by the writer at Santa Margarita, Trinidad, B. W. I. (June 15–20, 1942), resting in numbers on a single bush of *Cordia cylindrostachya*. Holotype male and allotype, U.S.N.M. No. 56691; paratypes in B.M.N.H. This species is distinguished by the shape of the aedeagus and of the posterior lobe of the pregenital sternite.

Genus CEDUSA Fowler

Cedusa FOWLER, Biologia Centrali-Americana, Rhynch. Hom., vol. 1, p. 112, 1904. (Genotype, *C. funesta* Fowler, designated by Muir, Bull. Hawaiian Sugar Planters' Exp. Stat., No. 12, p. 35, 1913.)

Vertex very short, scarcely produced before eyes, frons and clypeus rather narrow, about equal in length, with median carina; lateral margins subparallel, carinate, genae with a lamelliform subantennal process. Pronotum with carinae feeble or obsolete on disk, scarcely hollowed behind eyes, with an oblique transverse carina between eye and margin on each side, lateral lobes below this flat or nearly so. Mesonotum convex, very feebly tricarinate. Tegmina rather short and broad, dilated somewhat distad of apex of clavus, M leaving common stem at basal fifth, Sc + R forking at basal third, Cu₁ forking basad of apex of clavus.

CEDUSA CYANEA, new species

PLATE 10, FIGURES 182–190

Male: Length, 2.5 mm.; tegmen, 3.1 mm. Female: Length, 2.5 mm.; tegmen, 3.1 mm.

Vertex short, quadrate, much wider across base than long (3.3 to 1); apex straight, base shallowly emarginate, lateral margins slightly raised; frons twice as long as wide, apex 1.1 times as wide as base, lateral margins very slightly expanded below level of antennae, then very slightly incurved to suture; median carina present; a prominent subantennal process on genae, in front view about twice as long as antennae. Pronotum very short, anterior margin convex, posterior roundly emarginate, a thick carina between eye and tegula on each side, ventral lateral portions of pronotum not markedly bent anteriorly. Tegmina with M 5-branched at margin.

Head, pronotum, mesonotum, fore and middle legs, and genitalia dark fuscous; subantennal process, hind legs, and abdominal sclerites rather paler fuscous; abdominal membrane pale, sometimes tinged red medially; tegmina smoky brown, basal cell, a spot at base of stigma, a short transverse vein near apex of stigma, and an oblique line from apical fork of R to apex of clavus hyaline; veins slightly darker; wings hyaline, clouded pale fuscous, veins darker. Insect in life powdered a dusky blue.

Anal segment of male tubular, in dorsal view slightly longer than broad (1.2 to 1), exposed membranous portion rather broadly conical. Pygofer with lateral margins broadly sinuate, devoid of a median process ventrally. Aedeagus tubular, a broad twisted fold arising ventrally at base and curling to right side and upward at apex; a stout spine, deeply curved, directed dorsally and anteriorly at apex; on left side subapically and dorsally a flat lobe directed anteriorly with a short downward spine on its inner face distally; below this lobe a flat bladelike process directed anteriorly above dorsal surface of aedeagus, then twisted upward through 90° distally. Genital styles broad; in lateral view a short process on dorsal border near base, the tip of the process bent outward; inner margin simple, devoid of lobes.

Anal segment of female short, lateral angles not produced. Lateral styles simple, rather narrow, tapering bluntly to apex.

Described from 15 males and 9 females collected by the writer in St. John's Valley, Trinidad, B. W. I. (June 12, July 24, 26, 1942), resting on low bushes. Holotype male and allotype, U.S.N.M. No. 56692; paratypes in B.M.N.H. This species is distinguished by the shape of the anal segment of the male, of the genital styles, and of the aedeagus and by the dark color of the rostrum, legs, and abdomen.

CEDUSA RUBRIVENTRIS, new species

PLATE 10, FIGURES 191–194

Male: Length, 2.6 mm.; tegmen, 3.1 mm. Female: Length, 2.6 mm.; tegmen, 3.1 mm. Head, thorax, and tegmina as in *C. cyanea*.

Head and thorax dark fuscous; sclerites of abdomen and genitalia sometimes testaceous or fuscous; subapical joint of rostrum pallid, apical joint piceous; legs pallid or testaceous; membrane of abdomen crimson red; tegmina smoky brown, a spot at base of stigma, a short transverse vein near apex of stigma, and a narrow line from apical fork of Sc to apex of clavus hyaline; veins concolorous or slightly darker brown; wings hyaline, clouded fuscous, veins darker. In female first valvulae pallid or testaceous; insect in life powdered dusky blue.

Anal segment of male tubular, elongate, 2.4 times longer than wide at base, in dorsal view narrowing distally but expanding just before apex; membranous portion forming an elongated triangle medially. Pygofer with lateral margins very slightly sinuate, devoid of a median process ventrally. Aedeagus basally a simple tube; distally on left side of flexible portion a broad spinose process, angularly bent in middle, directed anteriorly in repose; mesad of this process and about as long, a membranous tube, sclerotized along its right side, terminating in two short falcate processes, one being rather blunt, the other spinose; on right side of flexible portion of aedeagus a sinuate spine directed obliquely upward, and distad of it a narrow, curved, bladelike process expanding into a flat blunt lobe at apex. Genital styles large, in ventral view with a blunt lobe on inner margin near base, then expanding and abruptly tapering toward exterior margin, which is produced at apex into a sharp point directed mesad.

Anal segment of female short. First valvulae of ovipositor with margins straight and almost parallel, bearing five spinose processes, long and slightly diverging.

Described from two males and two females taken by the writer in St. John's Valley, Trinidad, B. W. I. (June 12, 1942), resting on low bushes. Holotype male and allotype, U.S.N.M. No. 56693; paratype in B.M.N.H. This species is very like *cyanea* but is readily distinguishable by the shape of the male anal segment, genital styles, and aedeagus, and less easily in the female by the straight-sided first valvulae. In color it is distinguished by the pale subapical joint of the rostrum, the pale legs, the crimson abdomen, and in the female by the pale yellow first valvulae.

Genus PATARA Westwood

Patara Westwood, Trans. Linn. Soc. London, vol. 19, p. 13, figs. 6a–d, 1845.
(Genotype, *P. guttata* Westwood, *ibid.*)

Vertex small, triangular; frons very narrow, margins contiguous to near apex; vertex and frons in profile forming a curve; genae devoid of a subantennal process; antennae reaching beyond apex of head, second segment large, cylindrical, not compressed. Small, delicate species, exhibiting sexual dimorphism in the second segment of the antennae.

PATARA TRIGONA, new species

PLATE 10, FIGURES 195–201

Male: Length, 2.3 mm.; tegmen, 2.7 mm.

Antennae with second segment subcylindrical, expanding slightly to apex, uniformly minutely granular except at apex and along a narrow dorsal triangular area extending basad from apex. Tegmina with commissural margin only slightly excavated at apex of clavus.

Vertex, frons, genae, pronotum, and lateral areas of mesonotum fuscous; clypeus, rostrum, scutellum, and legs pallid; antennae yellow, clouded with very numerous minute piceous granules, bare portion pallid; eyes red; abdominal sclerites and genitalia pale fuscous, membrane red; tegmina fuscous, margin from middle of costa to apex of clavus white, apical veins white submarginally, claval vein distad of junction white to near apex, apical margin of tegmina tinged pink; wings hyaline, slightly suffused fuscous, veins darker.

Anal segment very short, subquadrate, posterior angles produced obliquely outward. Pygofer with lateral margins slightly sinuate, hind margin ventrally somewhat emarginate in middle, devoid of a medioventral process. Aedeagus tubular, bent dorsad apically, a small lobe on left dorsal margin two-fifths from base; two spines on left side toward apex, both directed anteriorly, the ventral spine at least 1.5 times as long as the dorsal; two longer spines on right side directed anteriorly, the lower sloping obliquely upward.

Described from one male taken by the writer in St. John's Valley, Trinidad, B. W. I. (June 12, 1942), resting on a low bush. Type, U.S.N.M. No. 56694. This species is distinguished by the bare triangular patch on the dorsoapical area of the second antennal segment, by the structure of the male genitalia, and by the color.

PATARA VITTATIPENNIS, new species

PLATE 10, FIGURES 202–207

Male: Length, 2.0 mm.; tegmen, 2.5 mm.

Antennae with second segment subcylindrical, expanding toward apex, uniformly minutely granular to apex, where it is bare in a circle around base of third segment. Tegmina with commissural margin distinctly and widely excavated distad of apex of clavus.

White or pallid; protarsi and mesotarsi very pale fuscous, membrane of abdomen red ventrally; tegmina hyaline, veins milky, costal cell fuscous basally, a distinct oblique pale fuscous band from middle of costal margin to anal angle, a paler band parallel to this from apical fork of Sc to tip of apical margin (cell M_1), a faint fuscous cloud submarginally in intervening apical cells, a faint oblique fuscous bar at apex of clavus, a second bar on the transverse vein between M and Cu_1, a fuscous band posterior and parallel to claval suture, an oblique band from junction of claval veins across Cu_1 then bent through 40° to lie horizontally between M and Cu_1, posterior claval vein bordered fuscous on each side basad of junction; wings hyaline.

Anal segment very short, subquadrate. Pygofer with lateral margins slightly sinuate, ventral margin straight, devoid of medioventral process. Aedeagus tubular, curved dorsad distally; on right side two short, broad bladelike pointed laminae arising at apex and directed anteriorly; on left side a long sinuate spine arising three-quarters from base and directed anteriorly, a second spine arising slightly distad of former, curving dorsad and somewhat anteriorly. Genital styles in lateral view narrow at base, expanding in basal two-thirds then narrowed to apex, which is bluntly rounded; a vertical granular fingerlike process on dorsal margin near base.

Described from one male collected by the writer in St. John's Valley, Trinidad, B. W. I. (Sept. 21, 1942), resting on a leaf. Type, U.S.N.M. No. 56695. This species is distinguished by its uniformly granulate antennae, by the distinctly excavated commissural margin of the tegmina, by the shape of the genitalia, and by the tegminal pattern.

PATARA POECILOPTERA, new species

PLATE 10, FIGURES 208–213; PLATE 11, FIGURE 214

Male: Length, 2.1 mm.; tegmen, 2.9 mm.

Antennae with second segment subcylindrical, expanding toward apex, four times as long as wide in middle, as long as mesonotum with scutellum, somewhat obliquely truncate at apex, uniformly minutely granular, except at apex and on a small round spot on dorsal surface near base. Tegmina with commissural margin not excavated distad of apex of clavus.

Vertex, genae below eyes, basal joint of antennae, basal part of clypeus, rostrum, posterior part of pronotum, mesonotum, pleurites, legs, and genital styles pale yellow; genae before eyes, distal part of clypeus, coxae, abdominal sclerites, anal segment, and pygofer pale fuscous; antennae dull yellow with a delicate piceous granulation; tegmina hyaline, clouded with fuscous, a series of six clear round spots on $Sc + R$, a spot on Sc beyond fork, followed distally by a large clear area extending across to R, three more spots before apical transverse vein, R with two clear spots near transverse vein, and an elongated spot basad of $Sc + R$ fork, a large clear area over common stem at base of tegmina, M with four clear spots on basal third, three in apical third, six clear spots in basal third of Cu_1, thence a spot at each veinal junction, a clear spot at junction of apical veins with margin; costal cell, transverse veins, and an oblique band near apex of clavus darker fuscous, veins mostly pale, anteroapical margin tinged reddish orange; wings hyaline, fuscous at base of anal area, veins fuscous.

Anal segment of male deflexed through 30° beyond anal opening, produced posteriorly into a narrow lobe. Pygofer with lateral margin broadly sinuate, devoid of medioventral process. Aedeagus tubular, directed upward distally to a flattened lobe; a spine on left side ventrally, directed anteriorly, a second spine, arising somewhat more dorsally, directed vertically then bent through 90° to point posteriorly; two large spines directed anteriorly from apical lobe, the upper short, the lower three-quarters as long as aedeagus. Genital styles narrow at base, expanding to an almost quadrate lobe at apex, a vertical process on dorsal margin at middle bearing at its tip two spines, one directed inward, the other outward.

Described from two males collected by the writer in St. John's Valley, Trinidad, B. W. I. (July 27, 1942). Type, U.S.N.M. No. 56696. This species is distinguished by the clear spot at the base of the second segment of the antennae, by the structure of the genitalia, and by the color pattern of the tegmina.

Family KINNARIDAE

The possession of wax-secreting plates on the terga of the sixth, seventh, and eighth abdominal segments is not a family character, unless *Prosotropis* and allied genera be separated into another family. The writer at present recognizes two subfamilies: KINNARINAE, including forms possessing such wax-bearing plates, and PROSOTROPINAE, including forms with them reduced on the sixth tergite, obsolete on the seventh, and absent from the eighth.

Subfamily KINNARINAE

BYTROIS, new genus

Vertex small, short, shallowly excavated basally, lateral margins greatly raised, strongly converging to level of middle of eyes, where they are joined by a short transverse carina; vertex in profile forming an unbroken curve with frons; frons narrow, deeply troughlike, lateral margins greatly elevated, gradually diverging to apex, apex about twice as wide as base, median carina absent, median ocellus distinct; frontoclypeal suture impressed; clypeus narrow, tumid, tricarinate; second segment of antennae more than twice length of first. Pronotum short, produced anteriorly into posterior emargination of head, shallowly excavate on hind border, median carina distinct, lateral carinae following hind margin of eyes, turning posteriorly between eyes and tegulae; mesonotum with disk flat, curved upward at scutellum, median carina distinct, lateral carinae somewhat less so. Hind tibiae unarmed, sometimes with eight or nine minute denticles. Tegmina with costal cell wide, Sc+R forking slightly before stigma, common stalk Sc+R+M fully two-thirds as long as basal cell; typically ten apical cells and an anteapical series of five cells, of which the anterior three are large; claval suture meeting commissural margin beyond middle of tegmen, clavus not granulate. Wings with third apical cell of M, a triangular cell, subequal in length to its stalk. Anal segment of male not bifid. Ovipositor incomplete.

Genotype: *Bytrois nemoralis*, new species.

BYTROIS NEMORALIS, new species

PLATE 11, FIGURES 221–229

Male: Length, 2.1 mm.; tegmen, 3.3 mm. Female: Length, 2.3 mm.; tegmen, 3.5 mm.

Vertex, frons, genae before antennae, lateral lobes of pronotum, pleura, procoxae and mesocoxae, and ventral sclerites of abdomen dark fuscous to piceous; clypeus, genae below antennae, basal segment of antennae, pronotum dorsally, mesonotum, protarsi and mesotarsi, postfemora, and abdominal tergites lighter fuscous; carinae of head and pronotum, second segment of antennae, and genitalia testaceous or pale fuscous; rostrum, profemora and mesofemora and tibiae, metatibiae and tarsi, and membrane of abdomen pallid.

Anal segment of male rather short, in dorsal view narrowed apically, slightly indented on posterior margin. Pygofer short, rather deep dorsoventrally, lateral margins excavated in upper half, produced into a blunt lobe at level of genital styles, ventral surface of pygofer tumid. Aedeagus short, consisting of a broad, short dorsal hoodlike lobe, flat above, curved downward laterally, with posterior margin sinuate, drawn out into a short point lateroapically, and below this a broad scooplike process, slightly longer than the dorsal hood, with a median ridge, minutely serrate, on its upper surface, and a corresponding groove on its lower. Genital styles short, broad, in side view to lower border sinuate, curving distally upward, the dorsal border mostly straight, turned slightly upward at apex, with a short vertical lobe subapically.

Anal segment of female small, lateral angles produced posteriorly almost as far as apex of telson. Lateral styles broad, lower margin rounded, dorsal margin deeply excavated, an expanded lobe, approximately quadrate, at apex. Ovipositor greatly reduced, largely membranous, with slender sclerotized components.

Described from 31 males and 44 females taken by the writer in St. John's Valley, Trinidad, B. W. I., on various dates between May 1942 and March 1943, on various shrubs and on cacao. Holotype male and allotype, U.S.N.M. No. 56697; paratypes in B.M.N.H. This genus differs from *Atopocixius* Muir, *Oeclidius* Van Duzee, and *Paroeclidius* Myers in not having the vertex produced in front of the eyes and in the details of the tegminal venation.

Subfamily PROSOTROPINAE

EPARMENOIDES, new genus

Head, with eyes, scarcely two-thirds width of pronotum; vertex longer than wide, shallowly excavated at base, lateral margins converging somewhat anteriorly, vertex in profile curving uninterruptedly onto frons, median carina distinct, no transverse carina at apex; frons one and three-quarters times longer than wide, apex about twice as wide as base, lateral margins diverging for two-thirds from base, then curving in toward suture, carinate, median carina distinct, percurrent, basal half of frons sloping evenly into vertex, distal half somewhat convex; median ocellus absent; clypeus at base not quite so wide as widest part of frons, tapering acutely to apex, carinate medially and laterally, somewhat convex; genae slightly tumid below antennae, devoid of a subantennal process; antennae with basal segment very short, second segment distinctly longer than broad; eyes moderately emarginate ventrally. Pronotum shorter than vertex, anterior margin incurved behind eyes, posterior margin shallowly excavated, median carina distinct, lateral carinae of the disk feebly present, a carina on each lateral margin between eye and tegula; mesonotum feebly convex, posteriorly concave, median and lateral carinae distinct, scutellum acute at tip. Hind tibiae unarmed. Tegmina slightly more than two and a half times as long as wide, seven apical cells, two ante-apical cells distad of nodal line; common stalk of $Sc+R+M$ about one-quarter length of basal cell, Sc+R forking close to stigma, anterior branch of M simple to apex; claval suture meeting commissural margin beyond middle of tegmen; clavus not granulate. Wings with veins of fourth apical cell without a common stalk at base, or with only a vestige. Anal segment of male bifid, the lateral lobes deflexed distally. Genital styles with a setose eminence on dorsal border behind apex. Ovipositor incomplete. Egg bluntly ovoid.

Genotype: *Eparmenoides ripalis*, new species.

EPARMENOIDES RIPALIS, new species

PLATE 11, FIGURES 215–220

Male: Length, 1.9 mm.; tegmen, 2.0 mm.   Female: Length, 1.8 mm.; tegmen, 2.0 mm.

Vertex testaceous, lateral carinae dark, a fuscous band transversely across middle, sometimes a pale line near each posterolateral angle; frons yellow, sometimes testaceous basally; clypeus very pale, genae pallid with a square black spot with its lower edge level with fronto-clypeal suture, first segment of antennae pale, second segment piceous, paler distally; pronotum testaceous, sometimes distinctly darker in anterior half, mesonotum narrowly fuscous anteriorly, otherwise testaceous, posterior margins and scutellum sometimes pallid; legs pallid; abdominal sclerites fuscous, membrane tinged red; tegmina yellowish, wings vitreous.

Anal segment of male deeply bifid, lateral lobes symmetrical, deflexed at apex. Pygofer with lateral margins sinuate, somewhat lobate in upper half. Aedeagus tubular, sharply upturned and tapering in apical half, a conical projection ventrally near base, an inner pair of slender processes curving upward and caudad, a longer pair of filamentous processes arising on upper margin about halfway from base, directed caudad and strongly upward, then looping forward, downward, and outward. Genital styles narrow, bent upward through 45° two-thirds from base, tapering to a point, with a rounded lobe on dorsal margin subapically.

Lateral styles of female deeply cleft, the dorsal lobe narrow and tapering, the ventral lobe almost ovoid in outline. Pregenital plate subquadrate, about one and a half times as broad as long.

Described from 12 males and 8 females taken by the writer in St. John's Valley, Trinidad, B. W. I. (July 27, 1942), feeding below leaves of *Cordia* sp. Holotype male and allotype, U.S.N.M. No. 56698; paratype in B.M.N.H. This genus differs from *Eparmene* Fowler in the shape of the frons and from *Quilessa* Fennah in the proportions of the frons and in the venation of the tegmina and wings.

Family DICTYOPHARIDAE

Subfamily DICTYOPHARINAE

Tribe DICTYOPHARINI

Genus LAPPIDA Amyot and Serville

Lappida AMYOT and SERVILLE, Histoire naturelle des insectes. Hémiptères, p. 505, 1843. (Genotype, *Dictyophara proboscidea* Spinola, Ann. Soc. Ent. France, ser. 1, vol. 8, p. 292, pl. 13, fig. 4, 1839 (as *Dyctiophora proboscidea*).)

Vertex with an elongate, narrow cephalic process, usually expanded at apex. Pronotum produced anteriorly, shallowly angularly emarginate on hind margin, tricarinate, lateral carinae diverging basad; mesonotum tricarinate, lateral carinae arcuate.

Protibiae elongated, distinctly exceeding length of profemora, posttibiae with four or five spines. Tegmina elongate, rather narrow, vitreous, with supernumerary longitudinal veins, and an apical, subapical and nodal line of transverse veins; stigma with three or four cells, sometimes fewer.

LAPPIDA species (?)

PLATE 11, FIGURES 230–234

Female: Length, 9.7 mm.; tegmen, 9.4 mm.

Vertex with a narrow groove medially, as long as eyes, a definite constriction before eyes, lateral margins raised, slightly rounded in profile; cephalic process expanded at tip; frons with lateral margins parallel, ampliate in apical third, converging to frontoclypeal suture. Pronotum with an impression on each side of median carina at middle, an oblique row of six granules followed by a row of three on each side. Profemora not toothed, posttibiae with five and six spines respectively. Stigma 2-celled.

Green; margins of cephalic process, lateral carinae of frons basad of ocelli, granulation of pronotum, marginal carinae of pronotum, and a line below them, apex of rostrum, apex of femora, a basal spot on protibiae, protarsi and mesotarsi, and anal segment dark fuscous to piceous, a red and black line along sides of cephalic process; tegmina yellowish, hyaline, stigma yellow, apical cells of M and Cu_{1a} infuscate, less so basad, veins brown; wings vitreous, veins fuscous.

Anal segment long, in side view expanding apically, obliquely truncate at apex. Ovipositor with first valvulae bearing six teeth on dorsal margin, second valvulae broad, greatly compressed laterally, sclerotized along outer margin near base, tapering evenly to apex, covered dorsally with a very thin foliaceous lobe narrowing abruptly to a slender point, third valvulae (lateral styles) rather broad, elongate, roundly tapering to apex, where there is a constriction followed by a short narrow appendage.

Described from a single female collected by F. W. Urich, Trinidad, B. W. I. (1919), taken from the collection of the former Imperial Department of Agriculture. It has not proved possible to place this specimen with accuracy owing to its poor condition. It is not represented in the collection of the B.M.N.H.

Genus TOROPA Melichar

Toropa MELICHAR, Abh. zool.-bot. Ges. Wien, vol. 7, p. 80, 1912. (Genotype, *Dictyophora ferrifera* Walker.)

Vertex quadrate, lateral margins parallel, basal margin angularly excavate, a transverse impression before eyes, at which vertex narrows into a cephalic process projecting obliquely upward, slightly expanded in apical third, rounded-truncate at apex, with lateral margins distinctly concave; frons with median carina present only in basal half, lateral carinae distinct throughout; clypeus tricarinate. Pronotum produced anteriorly, tricarinate, with an impression on each side of middle line; mesonotum tricarinate, lateral carinae arcuate. Protibiae not markedly longer than profemora, posttibiae with five spines. Tegmina long, rather narrow, with supernumerary longitudinal veins and an apical, subapical, and nodal line of transverse veins, stigma with three or four cells.

TOROPA FERRIFERA (Walker)

PLATE 11, FIGURES 243–250

Dictyophora ferrifera WALKER, List of specimens of homopterous insects in the collection of the British Museum, vol. 2, p. 313, 1851.

Male: Length, 11.3 mm.; tegmen, 13.9 mm. Female: Length, 12.0 mm.; tegmen, 15.0 mm.

Vertex with process nearly four times as long as wide at base, process directed upward at 35°; frons with median carina present only in basal half, lateral carinae reaching apex; cephalic process subrectangular in profile and in section. Hind tibiae with five spines. Tegmina with stigma with three or four cells.

Head, thorax, legs, and abdomen dark emerald-green; eyes dark red; lateral margins of cephalic process, dorsally and ventrally, lateral carinae of frons, pronotum behind eyes red, marginal carinae of pronotum between eyes and tegulae black in basal half, the carina below them on each side broadly black except on basal quarter. Tegmina hyaline, clouded with brown around apex, veins green, dark distad of nodal line. Wings hyaline.

Anal segment of male rather long, narrow, with upper margin, as seen in profile, almost straight, the lower somewhat curved, apex obliquely truncate. Aedeagus with periandrium narrow, tubular, elongate, deeply cleft laterally at apex; spines of penis arising from basal ring directed posteriorly to apex of periandrium, then recurving, the spine on left side straight, sloping obliquely ventrad, with a line of minute denticles on its upper surface, the spine on right side looping abruptly and sloping above periandrium to left side, then turning ventrad, minutely and somewhat sparsely corrugate near apex.   Genital styles triangular, expanding distally, obliquely truncate at apex, a rounded prominence on dorsal margin near base, a short curved spine at apex, a short triangular lobe projecting laterally near base.

Anal segment of female rather long, narrow, margins as viewed laterally diverging gradually distally, apex obliquely truncate. Pregenital segment with a median ventral lobe.   Ovipositor with first valvulae bearing four small and two large teeth dorsally with a broad deeply cleft lobe ventrally, second valvulae tubular narrowly sclerotized laterally, lateral styles elongate, rather narrow, dorsal margin almost straight, ventral margin curved, both narrowing distally to a constriction with a small triangular lobe distally.

Described from eight males and seven females taken by the writer, one female at St. Augustine (Dec. 5, 1935), the remainder at Santa Margarita, Trinidad, B. W. I., on various dates in August and September 1942, resting or feeding on bushes, including *Croton* sp. and bamboo.   W. E. China has compared Trinidad material with the type.

Genus HYALODICTYON Fennah

Hyalodictyon FENNAH, Proc. Biol. Soc. Washington, vol. 57, p. 86, 1944. (Genotype, *Dictyophara nodivena* Walker, Insecta Saundersiana, Homoptera, p. 37, 1858.)

Vertex produced into a more or less elongated conical process, flattened or nearly so dorsally, lateral margins carinate, converging apically, apex bluntly angulate or rounded, posterior border shallowly excavated, median carina present reaching to apex; frons elongate, narrow, with a percurrent median carina and lateral carinae, usually complete; clypeus tricarinate; pronotum produced anteriorly, tricarinate, with an impression on each side of middle line, devoid of granules, two carinae present laterally behind eye on each side; mesonotum tricarinate.   Protibiae moderately long, posttibiae with four to six spines.   Tegmina vitreous, with seven rows of irregular transverse veins beyond nodal line, devoid of transverse veins on clavus.

HYALODICTYON TRUNCATUM (Walker)

PLATE 11, FIGURES 235–238

Dictyophara truncata WALKER, List of homopterous insects in the collection of the British Museum, vol. 2, p. 316, 1858.

Vertex produced before eyes for more than twice their length, slightly more than 1.5 times as long as wide across base, lateral margins converging, more so just distad of eyes, rounded to apex distally; frons in profile slightly concave in middle, median and lateral carinae present, the latter incurved basally to meet at an acute angle; rostrum not reaching nearly to middle of porrect postfemora. Legs with protibiae rectangular, 25 times longer than width of their widest side at middle. Tegmina with stigma 4- to 7-celled.

Anal segment of female in side view with dorsal margin gradually and sinuately raised, apex obliquely truncate, lower margin shallowly curved, total length equal to width across base. First valvulae of ovipositor with four small and distally two large teeth on dorsal margin; lateral styles approximately ovoid, dorsal border shallowly curved, ventral border more strongly so, with a very short broad lobe on distal margin.

Described from six females, one collected by M. D. French-Mullen (Feb. 14, 1937), the remainder by the writer (July–Dec. 1942, on various dates) resting on bushes. A Trinidadian specimen was compared by Mr. China with the type.

HYALODICTYON FALLAX, new species

PLATE 11, FIGURES 239–242

Female: Length, 12.0 mm.; tegmen, 12.5 mm.

Vertex rather elongate, produced before the eyes for twice their length, shallowly excavate at base, median carina present, lateral margins straight, gradually converging apically, roundly incurved at apex; frons in profile flat, not concave, lateral margins parallel, lateral carinae very roundly arched, not at all angulate, at their basal junction; rostrum reaching posteriorly well beyond posterior coxae, base of last joint level with postcoxae, tip reaching almost to middle of porrect postfemora. Legs long and slender, protibiae rectangular in section, fully 32 times longer than wide across middle of widest side, or even more. Tegmina without cross veins on the corium, Sc + R forking near stigma, stigma with three cells, M forking about middle of tegmen, Cu$_1$ forking markedly basad of M fork.

Green, apex of rostrum piceous; tegmina hyaline, veins green; wings vitreous, veins pale.

Anal segment short, in dorsal view as broad as long, excluding telson, dorsal margin abruptly raised from base, passing straight to anal foramen, lower margin curved. Lateral styles of ovipositor broad, subtriangular, tapering distally, upper margin almost straight, lower margin curved. First valvulae with five rather slender spines on dorsal margin, passing into grooves at their bases, and two larger upturned spines apically.

Described from two females, one collected by F. W. Urich, Trinidad, B. W. I. (1921), the other by the writer in St. John's Valley, Trinidad,

B. W. I. (June 12, 1942).   Type, U.S.N.M. No. 56673.   This species is close to *H. truncatum* but is readily distinguished by the lateral margins of the cephalic process being straight, the vertex being proportionately narrower than in *truncatum*, by the frons in profile being straight, not slightly concave, by the lateral carinae of the frons being perfectly arched in a curve where they meet basally, not slightly angulate, by the distinctly more slender protibiae, and by the shape of the anal segment of the female.

Genus RETIALA Fennah

Retiala FENNAH, Proc. Biol. Soc. Washington, vol. 57, p. 83, 1944.   (Genotype, *R. proxima* Fennah, *ibid.*)

Vertex longer than broad (about 1.5 to 1), slightly curved upward anteriorly, basal margin shallowly excavated, lateral margins straight or very slightly convex between eyes, thence narrowing to apex in a straight line without an abrupt constriction in front of eyes, not quite meeting at apex, joining lateral margins of frons; sides of frons visible in dorsal view, and junction of lateral carinae of frons visible beyond apex of vertex, median carina feebly present on vertex, a short feeble carina at base on each side; frons narrow, longer than broad (about 2.5 to 1), widest at basal third, lateral margins sinuate, median carina percurrent, thick at base, narrowing apically, lateral carinae diverging as far as basal two-fifths, then sinuately converging to meet in middle line at apex, between these carinae frons somewhat tumid; clypeus narrow, tricarinate; rostrum reaching beyond postcoxae; antennae with basal segment short, second segment ellipsoidal, studded with sensory pits, the terminal segment inserted dorsally and exteriorly before apex of second.   Pronotum produced anteriorly in middle, posteriorly angularly emarginate, tricarinate on disk with the lateral carinae becoming obsolete basally, an impression on each side of middle line, two carinae at lateral margin of each side, between eye and tegula; two carinae on each tegula, mesonotum elongate, tricarinate, disk flat.   Legs long and slender, protibiae longer than profemora, posttibiae typically with four spines.   Tegmina rather long and narrow, $Sc+R+M$ stalk about half as long as basal cell, $Sc+R$ forking just before stigma, level with apex of clavus, M forking at middle of tegmen, Cu_1 forking at apical third of clavus, stigma with three cells, a nodal line and a subapical line of transverse veins present, R typically with three branches at apical margin, M with seven, Cu_{1a} with three, Cu_{1b} with two.

RETIALA VIRIDIS, new species

PLATE 11, FIGURES 251–264

Male: Length, 8.4 mm.; tegmen, 7.9 mm.   Female: Length, 8.3 mm.; tegmen, 8.3 mm.

Vertex longer than broad (1.4 to 1) ; frons longer than broad (2.6 to 1). Protibiae longer than profemora (1.4 to 1).

Bright green in life; lateral margins of vertex at apex, of frons at base, lateral carinae of frons at base, a pair of laterad spots at apex of each femur, apex of rostrum and posttibial spines black; protarsi and mesotarsi fuscous; tegmina vitreous, veins and stigma pale green; wings vitreous, veins pale yellow, becoming brown near apical margin.

Anal segment of male elongate, in lateral view expanding apically, sinuately truncate at apex with a small lip protruding posteriorly, anus subterminal. Pygofer with lateral margin bent posteriorly almost in a right angle, ventral margin transverse. Aedeagus with a short ringlike component at base, extended caudad ventrally and furcate at its apex, a large membranous fold, symmetrically biramous, with a sclerotized rod, arising from a median common stem, traversing the membrane on each side, each rod in ventral view being angularly S-shaped, and meeting its counterpart at apex; middle portion of aedeagus consisting of a flat elongated plate, stiffened with a pair of sclerotized rods, overlying a subrectangular membranous apodeme, laterally compressed and apically truncate.

Anal segment of female similar to that of male. Lateral styles broad, with margins subparallel, tapering somewhat abruptly near apex, with a setigerous area apicodorsally, a large shallowly domed thin flange projecting caudad dorsally joined to lateral portion at base; first valvulae with five very small teeth dorsally, passing into long grooves at their bases, and two large teeth apically, on inner aspect ventrally an elongate foliaceous lobe; second valvulae thin and pointed.

Described from five males and six females collected by the writer at St. Augustine, Trinidad, B. W. I., on various dates between July and December 1942 on Liberian coffee, *Casuarina*, and *Hibiscus*. Holotype male and allotype, U.S.N.M. No. 56699; paratype in B.M.N.H.

Genus TAOSA Distant

Taosa DISTANT, Ann. Mag. Nat. Hist., ser. 7, vol. 18, p. 355, 1906. (Genotype, *Flata suturalis* Germar, Ent. Arch. Thon, vol. 2, p. 48, 1830.)

Vertex short, not much exceeding eyes, at most as broad as long, usually much broader, rounded or truncate at apex, very shallowly excavated at base, lateral margins parallel between eyes, or very slightly converging, transverse carina at apex curved, a distinct triangular or quadrangular facet on each side of head distad of junction of lateral margins with transverse carina, vertex slightly depressed, median carina absent or scarcely present at base; frons not much longer than broad, lateral margins sinuate, expanding to below level of antennae, then curving inward to suture, median and lateral carinae present, the latter sometimes feeble; clypeus with a median carina and carinate lateral margins. Pronotum with anterior margin convex, posterior margin shallowly excavated, with a deeper median notch, median carina present; mesonotum tricarinate. Tegmina long and rather narrow, Sc+R forking near stigma, M forking basad of apex of clavus. Cu₁ forking still further basad, stigma with two to four cells, nodal line of transverse veins present, a subapical line which is, sometimes rather irregular, and an apical line, veins of clavus uniting before middle.

This genus is the same as *Cuernavaca*, a subgenus of *Dictyophara* erected by Kirkaldy with *Dichoptera herbida* Walker as its type (Kirkaldy, Bull. Hawaiian Sugar Planters' Assoc., Div. Ent., No. 12, p. 14, 1913). The species are most readily separated by the shape of the vertex, while the writer has made use of the genitalia, that of the first valvulae of the ovipositor being exceptionally useful.

TAOSA VITRATA (Fabricius)

PLATE 11, FIGURES 265–271

Flata vitrata FABRICIUS, Systema rhyngotorum, p. 48, 1803.
Cladodiptera viridifrons WALKER, Insecta Saundersiana, Homoptera, p. 41, 1858.

Vertex broader than long (1.7 to 1), not projecting before eyes, anterior margin weakly curved, triangular facet on each side apically distinct, base of frons visible from above; frons with median carina distinct, lateral carinae less so, frons about 1.7 times longer than wide. Posttibiae with four spines. Stigma of tegmina with two or four cells.

Dark brown; vertex pale, frons pale with a transverse piceous band across basal eighth, clypeus pale in basal half, piceous in apical half, rostrum pale greenish yellow, genae pale; pronotum pale anteriorly in middle, piceous anteriorly behind and below eyes, basal margin infuscate; mesonotum with two or three pairs of transverse brown spots on disk between median and lateral carinae, scutellum very pale, almost white; femora piceous on inner surface, protibiae and tarsi dark; abdomen dark brown, a pale broad longitudinal band medially on dorsal and ventral surfaces, lateral margins pale, genitalia fuscous; tegmina with veins of membrane very dark, nodal line of cross veins narrowly infuscate from R, a broad dark oblique line from apex of R to apex of clavus, with a second dark band arising at apex of R and following apical margin to Cu₁ₐ, commissural margin infuscate from apex of Cu₁ᵦ to a point halfway along clavus; wings with veins dark, anal area fuscous toward margin.

Anal segment of male rather short, dorsal margin in profile decurved, then passing straight to apex, lower margin curved, apical margin obliquely truncate. Aedeagus narrow, tubular, slightly expanding distally, then converging, with a bluntly rounded lobe projecting posteriorly on each side at apex, ventral border with a pair of triangular plates at apex, each with a spine projecting a short distance beyond it. Genital styles in side view subovate, strongly excavated on dorsal margin toward base, with a short decurved tooth directed outward at middle of excavation, and a second tooth pointed anteriorly just distad of it.

Described from one male specimen collected by Dr. J. G. Myers at Ocumare de la Costa, Venezuela (Dec. 17, 1930), and since sent to the British Museum.

Distant has synonymized *T. viridifrons* Walker with *T. virata* and Melichar gives the same synonymy. Melichar's description of *vitrata* does not agree with the original description, whereas his description of *suturalis* Germar agrees with Fabricius's description of *vitrata*, "caput atrum fronte rostroque fuscis: labio tamen atro. Thorax elevato lineatus, ater scutello apice fusco. Abdomen atrum margine fusco. Elytra hyalina margine postico fusco. Pedes fusci." W. E. China states that the type of *viridifrons* appears to be missing.

TAOSA BIMACULIFRONS Muir

PLATE 11, FIGURES 272–274; PLATE 12, FIGURES 275–277

Taosa bimaculifrons MUIR, Proc. Hawaiian Ent. Soc., vol. 7, p. 470, 1931.

Female: Length, 10.0 mm.; tegmen, 12.5 mm.

Length of vertex slightly more than half width at base, vertex not projecting before eyes, anterior margin shallowly curved, triangular facet on each side anteriorly distinct, lateral margins almost parallel, basal margin shallowly excavate; base of frons visible from above, carinae of frons distinct except at base. Hind tibiae with four spines. Stigma with three cells.

Green; a piceous quadrate spot overlying base of each lateral carina of frons; metanotum, a spot on metapleurites, protibiae and tarsi, metacoxae and trochanters dark brown; tegmina vitreous, veins greenish, dark on membrane distad of nodal line, stigma greenish brown, a fuscous semicircular spot extending over three cells at apical margin, and slightly overlapping into a further cell on each side; wings hyaline.

Ovipositor with first valvulae deflexed distally, then upturned apically, two recurved teeth on dorsal margin three-quarters from base, three much smaller teeth distad, directed posteriorly, and a pair of teeth at apex, curved upward, the distal tooth longer than the subapical tooth; second valvulae narrow, elongate, expanding before apex, rather deeply cleft at apex, the tip of each lobe pointed; lateral styles rather broad, dorsal margin shallowly concave, ventral margin convex, two processes at apex, directed caudad, a smaller process on apical margin below them, a broad thin lamina dorsally attached at base, horizontal, lying mesad of lateral portion.

Described from one female collected on the Amakura River, Venezuela, by Dr. J. G. Myers (February 1931). On p. 472 of his paper Muir states that the base of the frons visible in dorsal view is swollen in the middle in *bimaculifrons*, and elsewhere that a female allotype is deposited in the collection of the Hawaiian Sugar Planters' Association Experiment Station. On inquiry, Dr. C. E. Pemberton kindly informed the writer that no specimens of the genus could be found in the collection of the Station. W. E. China, to whom the matter was referred, stated that the type is not in the British Museum collection but that the collection does possess "a female paratype from Tena, Ecuador (F. X. Williams IV, 1923)." This paratype does not show the swollen frons, viewed from above, and it is possible that the description and figure were taken from the male type, in which case the character may be more pronounced in this sex. Myers's specimen is in the British Museum.

Of the species treated by Muir the British Museum does not possess specimens of *T. viridis* Muir, *T. lineatifrons* Muir, and *T. sororcula* Berg, or as already indicated, the type of *T. viridifrons* Walker.

TAOSA MULIEBRIS (Walker)

PLATE 12, FIGURES 278–283

Cladodiptera muliebris WALKER, List of specimens of homopterous insects in the collection of the British Museum, Suppl., p. 76, 1858.

Male: Length, 8.0 mm.; tegmen, 10.0 mm. Female: Length, 8.0 mm.; tegmen, 10.1 mm.

Vertex 1.7 times as broad as long, not projecting before eyes, lateral margins almost parallel, basal margin shallowly excavate, anterior margin shallowly curved, median carina present at extreme base; triangular facet on each side apically distinct; frons not much visible from above, carinae rather feeble, the lateral carinae curved, obsolete at base and at apex. Hind tibiae 4-spined. Stigma 2–3-celled.

Greenish brown; frons yellowish; legs dark testaceous, posttibiae banded fuscous, abdomen reddish at margin of segments; tegmina vitreous, stigma fuscous, a fuscous area distally on margin from apical veins of R to apex of clavus, this dark area straight on inner margin except for an indentation near middle, clavus fuscous between common stalk of united claval veins and commissural margin.

Anal segment of male rather short, dorsal margin in side view curved downward near base, then passing in a straight line to apex, lower margin curved, apex obliquely truncate. Aedeagus narrow, tubular, cleft dorsally at apex with each lateral lobe tapering to a point, curving somewhat mesad, and overlain by a thin membranous lamella, dorsally a pair of penial spines emerging subapically and abruptly recurved anteriorly. Genital styles subovate, dorsally excavated near base, with a tooth directed outward and downward and a second tooth directed anteriorly in basal half of upper margin.

Ovipositor with first valvulae rather broad, with four large curved teeth on dorsal margin in distal half, followed posteriorly by a row of four much smaller teeth; second valvulae in side view broad, with upper and lower margins convex, the former less so, a marked cleft at apex; lateral styles with dorsal margin straight or nearly so, the lower margin deeply curved, a narrow point at apex, a thin horizontal lamella lying mesad and attached at base.

Described from one male specimen taken at Yarikita, Northwest District, British Guiana (March 1931), and one female taken at Bom Jardim, Lower Amazon (Sept. 16, 1933), by Dr. J. G. Myers. The male specimen and drawings of the valvulae of the ovipositor were found by W. E. China to agree very well with Walker's type of *T. muliebris*, which is a female. Melichar synonymizes *T. muliebris* under *T. suturalis* Germar, but his description of *suturalis* does not agree with *muliebris*, whereas his description of *T. vitrata* (Fabricius) does so reasonably well. It is possible that there has been some confusion of *suturalis* and *vitrata*, and the writer believes that these names along with their synonymies should be transposed in Melichar's monograph.

TAOSA AMAZONICA, new species

PLATE 12, FIGURES 284-291

Female: Length, 9.3 mm.; tegmen, 12.0 mm.

Vertex wider across base than long (1.6 to 1), scarcely projecting before eyes, lateral margins slightly converging, anterior margin rather strongly curved, basal margin shallowly excavated, median carina feebly present on basal half, triangular facet anterolaterally distinct, base of frons visible from above; frons with carinae distinct, though feeble at base; hind tibiae with four spines; stigma with three cells.

Green; frons paler at base, lateral carinae of frons broadly overlain with a band of reddish brown in basal two-thirds, rostrum piceous at apex, vertex with a dark linear spot on each side of median carina, pronotum with a spot behind each eye, mesonotum with a brown spot anteriorly at apex of median carina, a spot immediately outside each lateral carina at apex, and a spot inside at base, a few dark suffusions laterad, pro- and mesotibiae and tarsi slightly infuscate; tegmina vitreous, veins green, fuscous between subapical line and margin, stigma green; wings vitreous, veins dark.

Anal segment subequal in length to hind tarsus, narrow, in side view parallel-sided, obliquely truncate at apex. Lateral styles narrow, almost as long as anal segment, gradually expanding distally, rounded at apex, a thin horizontal lobe dorsally, attached at base and lying mesad. First valvulae long, narrow, with a row of three small simple teeth three-quarters from base on dorsal border, with a sclerotized plate distally bearing on its dorsal border a row of 11 minute teeth, short and evenly spaced, each tooth bifid or notched at apex.

Egg elongate-oval, 0.23 by 0.91 mm., thin-walled, but slightly expanded into a thickened shallowly domed cap at one pole.

Described from two females collected by Dr. J. G. Myers at Arumanduba, Lower Amazon (Sept. 17, 1933). Type in B.M.N.H.; paratype, U.S.N.M. No. 56779. This species differs from the others in the shape of the vertex, being approached only by *T. herbida* (Walker) and *T. paraherbida* Muir in this character, and in the unusually long anal segment and ovipositor, as well as in the detailed structure of the valvulae.

TAOSA HERBIDA (Walker)

PLATE 12, FIGURES 292–302

Dichoptera herbida WALKER, List of specimens of homopterous insects in the collection of the British Museum, vol. 2, p. 306, 1851.

Male: Length, 9.0 mm.; tegmen, 11.8 mm. Female: Length, 9.1 mm.; tegmen, 12.0 mm.

Length of vertex two-thirds width across base, about one-third projecting in front of eyes, anterior margin rather strongly curved, lateral margins slightly converging anteriorly, basal margin shallowly excavate, median carina present basally; facet distinct on each side anteroapically, subquadrate rather than triangular, base of frons visible from above, distinctly swollen in middle between lateral carinae; frons with carinae not strongly present, lateral carinae feeble. Hind tibiae with four spines. Stigma usually 4-celled.

Green; a broad orange band overlying lateral carinae of frons in basal half, passing into black basally; apex of rostrum piceous, protibiae and tarsi fuscous, posttibial spines black. Tegmina vitreous, stigma green. Wings vitreous.

Anal segment of male in side view with dorsal margin curved downward slightly near base then passing straight to apex, lower margin shallowly convex, apex obliquely truncate. Aedeagus tubular with two ventral spinose processes arising subapically, directed posteriorly and obliquely upward, and two dorsal spines emerging at apex and abruptly recurved anteriorly. Genital styles somewhat elongate, lower margin convex, dorsal margin with two teeth at basal third, thence sloping concavely to apex, a small blunt lobe at apex produced posteriorly.

Anal segment of female short, in side view dorsal margin straight, lower convex, apex obliquely truncate. First valvulae each with two unequal rows of teeth dorsally, one row consisting of about eleven teeth, the other of about eight teeth, these being on a descending row arising near base of first. Second valvulae with a narrow, sinuate, sclerotized apodeme very obliquely truncate apically; below this a thin flange, obliquely truncate posteroventrally, with apical margin minutely serrate. Lateral styles with subparallel sides, the upper margin slightly concave, the lower convex, strongly curving upward to apex which is devoid of any process or lobe, a thin horizontal flange attached at base and lying mesad dorsally.

Described from three males and four females taken by the writer at St. Augustine, Trinidad, B. W. I., on various dates between May and November 1942 on Liberian coffee, and from one female collected by Dr. J. G. Myers at Ocumare de la Costa, Venezuela (Dec. 17, 1930).

TAOSA PARAHERBIDA Muir

PLATE 12, FIGURES 303–307

Taosa paraherbida Muir, Proc. Hawaiian Ent. Soc., vol. 7, p. 471, 1931.

Female: Length, 9.0 mm.; tegmen, 11.8 mm.

Vertex as long as broad across base, produced for about half its length in front of eyes, lateral margins parallel between eyes, basal margin rather shallowly angularly excavated, anterior margin strongly curved, median carina very feebly present at base, triangular facet anteroapically elongate; base of frons not visible from above, carinae of frons very feeble. Hind tibiae with four spines. Stigma with three cells.

Green; lateral carinae of frons overlain with a broad orange band, not black at base. Tegmina hyaline, stigma green. Wings hyaline.

Lateral styles of ovipositor rather narrow and elongate, dorsal margin in side view very shallowly concave, lower margin subparallel, curving upward to apex, which is not produced. First valvulae narrow, sinuate, with a row of eight stout, short, triangular teeth on dorsal margin, with a point at apex.

Described from a single female specimen collected by Dr. C. B. Williams on sugarcane (1921), no locality label being present. This specimen was taken from the collection of the former Imperial Department of Agriculture, in a group of miscellaneous insects collected in canefields, most of which bore a locality label, this being marked "Trinidad" in the great majority of cases. As *paraherbida* is known only from the mainland, it can only be classed on this evidence as a doubtful Trinidad record.

Family FULGORIDAE

7a. *Cephalic process absent.*
8a. *A single transverse carina between vertex and frons.*

Subfamily PHENACINAE

Genus PHENAX Germar

Phenax GERMAR, Rev. Ent. Silbermann, vol. 1, p. 175, 1833. (Genotype, *Fulgora variegata* Olivier.)

Vertex broader than long (4 to 1), quadrate, impressed on each side of middle, separated from frons by a single slightly curved carina, lateral margins elevated, basal margin shallowly excavate; frons broader at widest part than long, margins expanding sinuately and gradually to below level of antennae, then abruptly dilated and curved posteriorly to form a strong flange below antennae, the width of the frons at this level being twice its width at base, median carina present on basal half only, lateral carinae joined basally at middle at level of eyes, curving outward, downward, and then slightly inward to level of apex of median carina, then strongly diverging to suture, a short curved carina basally, directed distally, terminating at level of middle of eyes; clypeus almost equilaterally triangular, lateral margins curved sharply inward near suture, elevated middle portion of clypeus tumid, median carina present; antennae with first segment short, cylindrical, second segment globose, pitted with sensoria. Pronotum much broader than head, anterior margin of disk straight, posterior margin slightly convex, median carina present, lateral carinae diverging in a straight line to tegulae, lateral margins carinate between eye and lower margin of tegula on each side, ventrolateral margin of pronotum bent forward, forming a furrow; mesonotum more than twice as wide as long, devoid of median carina except at apex, lateral carinae obscure. Legs long, femora and tibiae rectangular, margins minutely setose, posttibiae with five or six spines. Tegmina expanding for two-thirds of length from base, apical margin very oblique, almost straight, coriaceous or papyraceous, Sc strong to middle, R forking at basal third, M and Cu_1 forking about basal quarter, transverse veins numerous beyond nodal line, regular, crescentically curved, occurring between all the supernumerary longitudinal veins. Wings densely reticulate.

PHENAX VARIEGATA (Olivier)

PLATE 12, FIGURES 308–310

Fulgora variegata OLIVIER, Encyclopédie méthodique: Histoire naturelle des insectes, vol. 6, p. 573, 1791.

Female: Length, 25 mm.; tegmen, 54 mm.

Frons about 3.5 mm. wide at base, 7.0 mm. wide at apex. Protibiae and mesotibiae one-fifth longer than femora.

Head yellowish brown, a piceous spot on vertex on each side of middle line, a piceous area between carinae on basal half of frons, distally two

:spots on each side between lateral carinae and margins, a piceous spot on each side of tumid area of clypeus basally, second segment of antennae dull fuscous; pronotum yellow-brown with two spots on callus of disk anteriorly, three large spots near posterior margin, four spots on each side behind lateral carinae, two spots on each side between upper carinae and the lower carinae of the lateral margin, two large elongated spots on lateral lobes below lateral carinae of margin; mesonotum pale brown, four small dark spots on each side close to anterior margin, a small spot on each side near base of scutellum; legs yellow, three dark zones on profemora and mesofemora and tibiae, a dark spot on posterior femora, three dark bands on posterior tibiae, protarsi and mesotarsi fuscous, metatarsi pale yellow; abdomen pale yellow; tegmina pearly yellow, translucent, barred with red and black between Sc and C in basal half, a series of narrow black bars running obliquely across most of basal half, with a more prominent group at midpoint of claval suture directed anteriorly to M, a distinct black and orange band, indented at middle, transversely between costa and apex of clavus, membrane beyond nodal line minutely transversely barred, a broad interrupted band of black and yellow-brown approximately parallel to apical margin, apical margin barred with about six dark spots; wings transparent, fuscous at margin ,with pale areas forming a broken submarginal line.

Insect powdered with fawn in life; the female sometimes bearing waxy filaments more than 3 cm. long at apex of abdomen.

Described from one female taken by Dr. J. G. Myers, at Wanaina, Northwest District, British Guiana (March 1931). Specimen in B.M.N.H.

8b. Two parallel carinae between vertex and frons, with a distinct groove between them; no carina or spine situated in front of eyes.

Subfamily POIOCERINAE

Tribe POIOCERINI

Genus SCARALIS Stål

Scaralis STÅL, Ent. Zeit. Stettin, vol. 24, p. 241, 1863. (Genotype, *Lystra picta* Germar, designated by Distant, Ann. Mag. Nat. Hist., ser. 7, vol. 18, p. 197, 1906.)

Vertex very short, five or six times as broad as long, apical margin shallowly curved anteriorly, lateral margins parallel or slightly indented, posterior margin broadly excavated, disk of vertex impressed; frons subquadrate, lateral margins subparallel, somewhat sinuate in basal half, ampliate in apical half, basal margin carinate with a groove between this and apical transverse carina of vertex, median carina incomplete, joined near middle of frons by a V-shaped ridge, sometimes incomplete, arising from basal and apical angles of frons on each side; frontoclypeal suture distinctly arcuate, deeply impressed; clypeus broadly triangular, with a tumid median area medially toward base; antennae with second segment globose; eyes not large, with a minute tooth posteriorly. Pronotum broad, slightly broader than head with eyes, approximately three times as long as vertex, anterior margin strongly convex, posterior margin shallowly excavate, median carina present, though usually not complete, sometimes joined by a transverse callus or ridge on each side; mesonotum broad, tricarinate, the lateral areas variously ornamented by calloused elevations or ridges; scutellum thickened. Tegmina with sides subparallel, obliquely truncate at apex, costal cell rather narrow, veins basad of nodal line prominent, with transverse veins irregular, numerous supernumerary longitudinal veins distad of nodal line with transverse veins in simple ladderlike series; clavus with veins uniting near their junction with commissural margin. Hind tibiae with four or five spines. Abdomen with last visible segment with tergite broadly rounded posteriorly, produced above anus.

SCARALIS SEMILIMPIDA (Walker)

PLATE 13, FIGURES 326–329

Poiocera semilimpida WALKER, List of specimens of homopterous insects in the collection of the British Museum, vol. 2, p. 300, 1851.

Head, pronotum, mesonotum, procoxae, and mesocoxae brown or dark testaceous; a small median spot anteriorly on vertex, an elongate spot on each side of frons basally, a large spot on each side of middle line at level of antennae, a median spot on clypeus at base black; pronotum with a median spot apically, a cloud behind eyes extending laterad into a spot, a round spot on each side of middle of disk, a round spot on lateral lobe below antennae piceous; mesonotum with two large spots touching middle line in middle of disk, two spots anterolaterally, two large spots posterolaterally, a small spot on each side at base of scutellum dark fuscous or piceous; a small dark cloud below insertion of tegmen, with a large dark spot on pleurite below it, and a spot near base of procoxae and mesocoxae; legs reddish, tarsi dark; abdomen red; tegmina with costal vein red, remainder mostly yellow, transverse veins red basally, pale in a median transverse band, distad of this pale reddish orange to nodal line, intervenal areas black, reddish in a median transverse band, four pale spots in costal cell, about six paler spots in pale transverse area, and about six pale spots on clavus, transverse veins narrowly pale at base of membrane, darker distally, longitudinal veins fuscous; wings vitreous with a large area of crimson-red and black at base, veins dark.

Lateral styles of ovipositor expanding distally, bluntly rounded apically, a short spine, directed posteriorly, on dorsal margin at apex, apical margin setose; first and second valvulae thin, membranous, rather narrow, with sides subparallel, the former consisting of two lobes, the dorsal pointed apically, the ventrolateral obliquely truncate, the second valvulae simple, rounded apically.

Described from two females taken by Dr. J. G. Myers on the Upper Essequibo River, British Guiana (Nov. 22, 1935). One specimen in B.M.N.H., the other in the collection of the Imperial College of Tropical Agriculture, Trinidad. W. E. China has indicated that the above differ from British Museum material in the presence of fuscous suffusions over the red area at the base of the wings, but states that *semilimpida* is a somewhat variable species.

7b. *Cephalic process present, directed anteriorly.*

Subfamily FULGORINAE

Genus LATERNARIA Linnaeus

Laternaria LINNAEUS, Museum Ludovicae Ulricae Regiae, p. 152, 1764. (Genotype, *Cicada laternaria* Linnaeus, Systema naturae, ed. 10, vol. 1, p. 434, 1758, fixed by tautonymy.)

Trinidad specimens examined by the writer fall into two species agreeing reasonably with *L. laternaria* Linnaeus, as interpreted by Da Fonseca and more doubtfully with *L. servillei* Spinola as interpreted by him. The writer feels constrained to leave these species unnamed for the present; figures are given of their male and female genitalia (pl. 12, figs. 316, 319, 320–325, respectively).

Genus CATHEDRA Kirkaldy

Cathedra KIRKALDY, Entomologist, vol. 36, p. 179, 1903. (Genotype, *Phrictus serrata* (Fabricius) Stoll, Natuurlyke en narr't Leeven Naauwkeurig ... Cicaden, pl. 29, figs. 170 and A, 1788.)

Vertex produced anteriorly into a simple elongated cephalic process, hexagonal in section, directed anteriorly for most of its length, curved upward near apex, a short blunt spine above and below posterior half of eyes, a stout spine a short distance before eyes, a pair of spines dorsally about middle of cephalic process and a second pair, directed obliquely upward, near apex; frons with a row of eight or nine spines along each lateral margin, lateral carinae of frons with a similar row of nine spines, the anterior (basal) spine minute and the posterior five crowded, median carina distinct, lateral margins of frons excavated near antennae, a deep impression near frontoclypeal suture; clypeus rather small, slightly tumid with median carina percurrent and lateral margins raised; antennae set in a narrow rim, first segment short, cylindrical, second globose. Pronotum with anterior and posterior margins nearly straight, an impression on each side of median carina on disk, an undulate carina on each side between eye and middle of tegula, lateral margins carinate between lower side of eye and of tegula; mesonotum with median carina distinct, three shallow indentations on each side separated by a series of calloused ridges. Hind tibiae with about six spines. Tegmina with Sc strong in basal half, a short R+M stalk as long as basal cell, apical half of tegmina with about 32 rows of horizontal veins, joined by numerous arcuate cross veins. Wings with apical half closely reticulate, a broad and fairly deep excavation at posterior end of apical margin.

CATHEDRA SERRATA (Fabricius)

PLATE 12, FIGURES 311–315

Fulgora serrata FABRICIUS, Species insectorum, vol. 2, p. 313, 1781.

Vertex, including dorsal surface of process, greenish brown, frons purplish brown near tip of process and between lateral carinae and lateral margins, pale yellowish brown medially near clypeus, clypeus pale yellowish brown, antennae pale at base, fuscous apically, eyes reddish brown. Pronotum pale tawny, fuscous laterally at level of antennae, pale mossy green between indentations of disk, and on posterior and ventrolateral margins, with a few dark spots near tegulae. Legs pale tawny banded with fuscous. Thorax and abdomen pale ventrally. Tegmina fawn brown, translucent, suffused pale green along Sc and across base of clavus, suffused pink over R, M, and Cu₁ as far as nodal line, and over apex of clavus, a delicate irregular mottling of brown over whole of corium and membrane, an obscure band of brown from middle of clavus to Sc just distad of middle. Wings very dark, piceous or purplish, narrowly pale on anterior margin near base, a large orange-brown circle occupying most of apex, sparsely flecked in anteroapical quadrant with short pallid lines, a line of sparse pale dashes along anteroapical margin, apical angle shaded piceous.

Anal segment of female tubular, the foramen directed upward, lower surface flattened near base with margins raised, tumid apically with margins obscure. First valvulae of ovipositor broad at base, with a strong spine at apex with a strongly sclerotized ridge ventrally at its base; second valvulae narrow at base, dorsal margin sclerotized, straight, apex membranous slightly decurved, ventrally a deep membranous lobe; lateral styles broad, expanding distally, apical margin truncate, a thin dorsal horizontal lobe lying mesad, attached at base.

Described from two females collected by A. P. Blair, in Maraval, Trinidad, B. W. I. (April 28, 1941), and by F. Melizan in forest, Northern Range, Trinidad (March 1942).

Family ACHILIDAE

9a. Vertex very short, much broader than long, anterior margin straight.

Subfamily APATESONINAE

Genus ATESON Metcalf

Ateson METCALF, Bull. Mus. Comp. Zool., vol. 82, p. 369, 1938. (Genotype, *Ateson marmoratum* Metcalf, *ibid.* p. 370.)

Vertex short, about five or six times as broad as long, anterior margin straight; frons longer than broad, lateral margins subparallel, scarcely wider at level of antennae than at base, raised, forming a percurrent flange with raised margins of clypeus, disk of frons between raised lateral portions flat, median carina present, rather feeble, percurrent; antennae with second segment short, cylindrical, expanded at apex. Pronotum short, with median and lateral carinae, the latter diverging posteriorly; mesonotum tricarinate, with disk ovate, tegulae large. Tegmina tectiform, costal and commissural margins subparallel, membrane expanded beyond apex of clavus, apical margin bluntly rounded. Sc weak, with several branches to margin at apex, R simple as far as transverse line of cross veins, M with six or seven branches before transverse veins, Cu_1 forking at level of junction of claval veins, claval veins uniting about three-quarters from base, and joining truncated apex of clavus. Posttibiae unispinose.

ATESON CONSIMILE, new species

PLATE 13, FIGURES 330–335

Female: Length, 4.8 mm.; tegmen, 7.1 mm. Length to apex of tegmen, 8.0 mm.

Vertex five times as broad as long in middle; frons with median carina distinct, strongly so apically, but very feeble, and transversely notched, at extreme base; clypeus broadly tumid in middle, devoid of median carina. Pronotum in middle as long as vertex on the same line, a small callosity present on each side, carinae distinct; mesonotum with disk exactly twice as long as wide, tricarinate, median carina raised into a vertical flange, shallowly curved in profile. Tegmina with two small cells at apex of Sc, with a small elongate triangular cell basad of them on costal margin, R simple to apex, M with seven branches reaching apex, both branches of Cu_1 simple to apex, subapical line of transverse veins complete to hind margin near anal angle, the vein joining R and M very short, reduced to a thick spot between the almost contiguous veins; tegmina finely rugulose between veins.

Vertex testaceous, fuscous near lateral margins, frons testaceous, lateral basal angles fuscous, a fuscous band at margins, narrowly bordered piceous on inner edge distad of level of antennae, clypeus testaceous, fuscous laterally, rostrum fuscous, genae testaceous, sides above eyes fuscous; pronotum fuscous with a row of four ochraceous spots behind eyes and a few such spots on pronotum below eyes, mesonotum dark fuscous, a paler line near tegulae, a small ochraceous spot at base of lateral carinae and at tip of scutellum; legs fuscous; abdomen dark fuscous dorsally, pale ventrally, membrane pallid, genitalia fuscous; tegmina fuscous, darker on costal area and in a broad band across clavus just beyond middle, corium sprinkled with ochraceous spots, veins marked with spots throughout, a very pale rounded spot before stigma, membrane broadly and irregularly clouded with dark fuscous between stigma and apex of clavus, with sparse irregular ochraceous markings, subapical line, apical margin, and apical third of claval cells hyaline or pallid, a dark fuscous band traversing middle of apical cells parallel to margin, a darker fuscous spot in one cell at anterior apical angle; wings fuscous, veins dark except $M\text{-}Cu_1$ cross vein, and fork of Cu_1, which are hyaline.

Anal segment of female short, ringlike, telson thick, flattened, broadly semiovately rounded. Lateral styles of ovipositor broad, subquadrate, membranous part of apical margin narrow, with its basal edge subparallel to margin, a pointed membranous filament dorsally at apex; first valvulae strongly curved downward distally, with a small tooth dorsally at apical third, and two large sickle-shaped teeth subapically. Pregenital segment with posterior margin straight.

Described from one female collected by F. W. Urich, Verdant Vale, Trinidad, B. W. I. (January 1912). This species is distinctly smaller than the others of the genus; it differs from *marmoratum* Metcalf in the proportions of the vertex and from both *marmoratum* and *fuscum* Metcalf in details of tegminal venation and in color, occupying in the latter respect an intermediate position between Metcalf's species. The ovipositor is of the characteristically achilid pattern. Type, U.S.N.M. No. 56700.

9b. *Vertex not very short, not more than three times as broad as long, anterior margin more or less convex.*

Subfamily ACHILINAE

Genus PLECTODERES Spinola

Plectoderes SPINOLA, Ann. Soc. Ent. France, ser. 1, vol. 8, p. 328, 1839. (Genotype, *Flata collaris* Fabricius.)

Vertex between basal angles three times length in middle, lateral margins slightly converging distally, anterior margin carinate, distinctly convex, posterior margin broadly excavated, vertex projecting in front of eyes for half its length, its base on middle line anterior to middle of eyes, median carina present, obsolete apically; frons only a little longer than wide, strongly curved, lateral margins expanding to level of antennae, then incurved to suture, median carina percurrent, lateral margins°produced above genae; clypeus with a median carina and lateral margins carinate. Pronotum very short, not more than half length of vertex; mesonotum large, tricarinate, lateral carinae diverging posteriorly, tegulae rather large. Hind tibiae with one spine two-fifths from base. Tegmina with costal margin slightly recurved, a short $Sc+R+M$ stalk two-thirds as long as basal cell, $Sc+R$ fork level with fork of Cu_1, both slightly distad of junction of claval veins, costal cell of almost same width throughout.

PLECTODERES COLLARIS (Fabricius)

PLATE 13, FIGURES 336–343

Flata collaris FABRICIUS, Systema rhyngotorum, p. 53, 1803.

Female: Length, 4.3 mm.; tegmen, 6.0 mm.

Vertex broader than long in middle (3 : 1); frons curved through 100°; head, with eyes, about as wide as pronotum. Pronotum with median carina short, lateral carinae diverging to reach posterior margin level with inner border of eyes. Tegmina with a row of six small cells, arising from Sc and R between stigma and apical angle, M with three branches reaching margin, Cu_{1a} and Cu_{1b} simple to apex, a series of six subapical cells, the first and sixth elongate, the third triangular, smaller than the remainder.

Piceous; a narrow line inside each lateral margin of vertex, a narrow border on basal margin of pronotum, a broad band across middle of clypeus, on genae below antennae, across lateral lobes of pronotum, covering base of procoxae, pleurites below tegmina, tegulae, inner margin of tegmina, veins of basal cell yellow, and posterolateral margins of mesonotum, where its inner edge is tinged with red; costal cell dull orange-yellow, brighter near stigma, wings smoky; legs fuscous, posttibiae narrowly margined yellow.

Anal segment of female ovate. Ovipositor with first valvulae bilobed; a ventral lobe sclerotized at base, obliquely truncate apically, with a setigerous margin, overlain by a transparent membranous triangular plate; a dorsal lobe with upper margin with three teeth three-quarters from base, and two large spines at apex, lower margin membranous curved upward to a hooked process apically; second valvulae narrow, with lower margin almost straight, upper produced into a vertical lobe subapically; lateral styles broad, lower margin sinuate, dorsal margin strongly decurved, apex blunt.

Described from two females collected on the Amakura River, Venezuela, by J. G. Myers (February 1931). One specimen sent to B.M.N.H.

Genus KOLOPTERA Metcalf

Koloptera METCALF, Bull. Mus. Comp. Zool., vol. 82, p. 371, 1938. (Genotype, *Koloptera callosa* Metcalf.)

Vertex strongly produced before eyes, about twice as long as wide at base, median carina distinct, lateral margins converging distally, rounded apically to middle, disk flat; frons more than one and a half times as long as wide, lateral margins somewhat ampliate below level of antennae, median carina distinct; clypeus approximately half as long as frons, carinate medially and on margins, a short horizontal carina between eyes and lateral margins of frons, frons in profile very slightly concave, clypeus slightly tumid; antennae with second segment subglobose; eyes somewhat elongated anteroposteriorly. Pronotum short, anterior and posterior margins subparallel, median and lateral carina present on disk, three carinae between lateral carinae of disk and lateral margins, lateral margins carinate, with a subparallel carina ventrad. Mesonotum broader than long, tricarinate, median carina feeble posteriorly, lateral carina slightly diverging posteriorly. Tegmina rather narrow, anterior and posterior margins subparallel, a distinct fold on costal margin at node, with a callosity in apical cell on each side of it, Sc+R forking approximately level with junction of claval veins, M. simple to nodal line, Cu_1 forking basad of apex clavus, transverse line of cross veins between Sc and Cu_{1b} very short, R with two branches at apical margin, M with three, Cu_{1a} and Cu_{1b} simple to apex, curving anteriorly just distad of apex of clavus. Hind tibiae unispinose submedially.

KOLOPTERA CALLOSA Metcalf

PLATE 13, FIGURES 344–351

Koloptera callosa METCALF, Bull. Mus. Comp. Zool., vol. 82, p. 372, 1938.

Male: Length, 4.0 mm.; tegmen, 4.3 mm. Female: Length, 4.2 mm.; tegmen, 4.6 mm.

Fuscous, speckled with ochraceous spots; two darker bands across vertex, a fuscous cloud across frons basally, apical part of frons pale yellow, clypeus, and ventral half of body sometimes pale, sometimes slightly infuscate, legs tinged fuscous. Tegmina pale fuscous, speckled ochraceous; wings smoky.

Anal segment of male short, broad, truncate at apex. Pygofer short, a pair of elongated triangular plates on posterior margin medioventrally directed posteriorly. Aedeagus complex; periandrium in form of a narrow sclerotized ring basally, produced posteriorly on its ventral margin in a narrow stalk, widening distally and bearing at apex four spines, two directed anterolaterally on each side; arising from basal ring laterally and dorsally and connected with sclerotized ventral plate a wide membranous tube, flattened and somewhat depressed dorsally, with dorsolateral margins curled upward and mesad, beset with a row of six strong teeth recurved anteriorly, a deep cleft on each side apically between ventral plate and lateral borders and a deeper cleft between lateral borders and dorsal median lobe; penis consisting of two apodemes, narrow, tubular, approximated at base, separating distally, each with an oblique spine terminally. Genital styles rather elongate-ovate, with a prominent lobe in middle of dorsal margin, slightly incurved, and bearing four short curved teeth; on inner face basally a long slender curved process, truncate apically.

Ovipositor with lateral styles broad, dorsal and ventral margins strongly and about equally curved to meet in a point at apex, apical membrane triangular, extending farther along ventral margin than along dorsal; first valvulae with two small spines on dorsal margin two-thirds from base, two long spines at apex, a large triangular lobe ventrally, underlain by a short thick triangular setigerous lobe.

Described from one male and one female collected by the writer in St. John's Valley, Trinidad, B. W. I. (June 12, 1942, July 3, 1943).

Genus CATONIA Uhler

Catonia UHLER, Proc. Zool. Soc. London, 1895, p. 61. (Genotype, *Catonia nava* Say, designated by Van Duzee, Check list of the Hemiptera of America north of Mexico, p. 79, 1916.)

Vertex rather short, approximately one and a quarter times as wide across basal angles as long in middle, more or less excavated dorsally, lateral margins between eyes subparallel or slightly converging, distally curving mesad, posterior margin shallowly but distinctly excavated, median carina present in basal half; frons scarcely longer than wide at widest part, lateral margins expanding to below level of antennae, then curved in to suture, slightly elevated, a transverse carina at base, which together with convergent lateral carinae of vertex bounds a triangular areolet on each side, frons in profile slightly curved, median carina distinct, percurrent; clypeus not so wide as frons at widest part, tricarinate, slightly tumid near middle, about as long as frons; antennae small, second segment globose. Pronotum short, less than half length of vertex, anterior margin convex, transverse across disk, posterior margin broadly excavate, disk tricarinate, lateral carinae diverging posteriorly, a series of five weakly bordered depressions on each side of disk, and a larger areolet between eye and tegula on each side; mesonotum tricarinate, lateral carinae diverging slightly posteriorly. Tegmina elongate, costal and commissural margins subparallel, slightly broader beyond apex of clavus, Sc + R fork at or near middle, basad of apex of clavus, M with three branches before line of transverse veins, Cu_1 forking before middle. Hind tibiae with a single spine two-fifths from base.

CATONIA PALLIDA, new species

PLATE 13, FIGURES 352–361

Female: Length, 4.4 mm.; tegmen, 5.2 mm.

Head, with eyes, not quite so wide as pronotum, vertex produced for almost half its median length before eyes, wider across basal angles than long in middle (1.4:1), frons longer than broad (1.2 to 1). Tegmina with Sc+R fork approximately two-fifths from base, nine apical cells posterior to stigma, a subapical series of six cells, the first and sixth elongate, the third shortest, triangular.

Vertex fuscous, dappled thickly with minute pale spots, a larger pale spot near each end of lateral margins, areolets pale with a few minute dark specks; frons and clypeus sprinkled with pale spots, genae fuscous, pale near areolets of vertex, dappled with pale spots before eye, pale anteriorly below ocelli, antennae fuscous, apex of second joint pale, eyes dark red; pronotum dark fuscous on disk and sides, dappled with pale spots, areolar depressions fuscous with a pale spot in middle, bounded by pale interareolar ridges, mesonotum dark fuscous on disk, dappled with pale spots, markedly paler outside lateral carinae, tegulae pale dorsally, darker and mottled laterally; legs fuscous, profemora and mesofemora pale at base and apex, protibiae and mesotibiae pale at base, with a pale transverse band about one-third from base; abdomen fuscous, tinged with crimson laterally; tegmina pale testaceous, veins pale with a row of pale spots along each side, an oblique fuscous band, spotted pale, from costal margin to apex of basal cell, about nine dark patches on costal margin before stigma, a very broken band of fuscous from stigma to apex of clavus, a narrow dark area overlying Sc+R and Cu_1 and M near base, claval veins heavily and evenly barred with fuscous spots, membrane slightly smoky; wings smoky, veins dark.

Ovipositor with lateral styles subquadrate, apical margin rounded, somewhat indented near ventral angle, membranous area with inner edge subparallel to outer; ventrally a thin triangular membranous process, underlain by a sclerotized triangular setigerous lobe approximated to its counterpart along middle line; upper lobe of first valvulae with a sclerotized dorsal margin bearing a compact group of three teeth three-quarters from base, then curving downward and upward into a prominent curved apical spine with a smaller spine at its base; second valvulae converging toward middle line, in profile bulbous dorsally and ventrally at base, tapering to apex with a broad vertical membranous lobe dorsally on apical third.

Described from one female taken by the writer in St. John's Valley, Trinidad, B. W. I. (July 12, 1942). Type, U.S.N.M. No. 56701.

CATONIA PALLIDISTIGMA, new species

PLATE 13, FIGURES 362–368

Female: Length, 4.3 mm.; tegmen, 5.0 mm.

Head including eyes not quite so wide as pronotum; vertex produced about one-third of its median length before eyes, wider across basal angles than long in middle (1.4:1), hollowed out, median carina present on basal third; frons scarcely longer than wide. Tegmina with Sc+R fork about middle, a series of 11 apical cells distad of stigma, six subapical cells, the third smallest, triangular.

Vertex very pale, a fuscous mark basad of each areolet, a larger dark spot at each basal angle, areolets pallid, a pair of spots in depression of each; frons fuscous, a broad pale band transversely just basad of middle, extending on to genae to eyes, lateral margins regularly barred with fuscous and pale spots alternately; clypeus fuscous with a transverse pallid band across base, extending on to genae, and a smaller transverse band near apex; antennae with second segment pale fuscous, pallid at apex, eyes brown, mottled fuscous; pronotum with disk, carinae, and margins of areolets pale, depressions of areolets, and a small spot between carinae of disk fuscous; mesonotum dark fuscous, carinae paler, a pale linear spot at middle of median carina, two pale spots on each lateral carina, a distinct pale area just behind each tegula, a minute pale spot on each margin of scutellum near tip; profemora and mesofemora fuscous, pale at base and apex, with a pale spot two-thirds from base, postfemora fuscous, paler on inner surface, protibiae and mesotibiae fuscous, pale at base and apex, with a pale spot one-third from base, posttibiae pale fuscous externally, pallid apically and basad of spine, except for a narrow oblique fuscous bar, spine pale; abdomen fuscous, a series of testaceous spots lateroventrally, membrane red dorsally, pale ventrally; tegmina chiefly pale, with fuscous bars, costal margin evenly marked with oblique fuscous spots, a broad fuscous band from inner margin of clavus across to Sc+R, then distally between Sc+R and Cu₁ to join a diffuse dark area lying between node, apex of clavus, and sutural angle, veins pale, barred with fuscous dots, membrane suffused fuscous, speckled paler, veins on membrane very pale, transparent; wings smoky, veins concolorous.

Ovipositor with lateral styles subquadrate; first valvulae with a sclerotized dorsal margin bearing two, possibly three, small teeth three-quarters from base, then curving ventrally and finally upward into a prominent curved apical spine with a smaller spine at its base, ventrally a thin flat lobe tapering distally, underlain by a short sclerotized subtriangular setigerous lobe pointed distally; second valvulae narrow, converging apically.

Described from one female collected by Dr. J. G. Myers, Trinidad, B. W. I. (January 1932).   Type, U.S.N.M. No. 56702.

OPSIPLANON, new genus

Head, with eyes, not quite so wide as pronotum; vertex flat, not hollowed out, produced almost half its median length before eyes, twice as wide across basal angles as long in middle, lateral margins carinate, longer than middle line, strongly converging anteriorly in a straight line, or nearly so, median carinae strongly present throughout, posterior margin shallowly excavated; frons rather longer than wide at widest part, flat or scarcely tumid, somewhat curved in profile, lateral margins diverging to below level of antennae then curving inward to suture, median carina distinct, percurrent, lateral margins slightly elevated, a transverse carina at base, which with lateral carinae of vertex and margins of frons enclose a small triangular areolet on each side; clypeus about as long as frons, slightly tumid, with median and lateral carinae; antennae small, second segment subglobose.   Pronotum short, anterior margin convex, posterior margin broadly excavated, disk with median and lateral carinae, anterior margin carinate behind eyes, with three carinae to posterior margin, lateral margins carinate, with a carina below them; mesonotum tricarinate, lateral carinae diverging posteriorly.   Tegmina rather narrow, costal and commissural margins parallel to apex of clavus, membrane somewhat expanded distally, fork of $Sc+R+M$ one-seventh from base, $Sc+R$ fork at nodal line, or very near it, M forking at nodal line, with three branches reaching apical margin, Cu_1 forking level with apical quarter of clavus, claval veins joined distally by an oblique cross vein, a series of nine apical cells distad of apex of costal cell, a series of six subapical cells, the first small, trapezoidal, the third small, triangular.   Wings with R simple to apex, six apical cells before Cu_1.   Posttibiae with a single spine in basal half.

Genotype: *Opsiplanon ornatifrons*, new species.

OPSIPLANON ORNATIFRONS, new species

PLATE 13, FIGURES 369–374; PLATE 14, FIGURES 375, 376

Female: Length, 3.2 mm.; tegmen, 3.1 mm.

Vertex testaceous, median carina and lateral margins pale yellow, edged narrowly fuscous, a fuscous spot one-third from base along each lateral margin, areolets fuscous, margins pale, frons dark testaceous, narrowly fuscous at margins and across middle, basal margin pallid, three small pallid spots on lateral margins in basal half, the lowest extending on gena to ocellus of each side, a short pallid bar transversely on middle of frons level with second lateral spot, not reaching to lateral margins, clypeus narrowly and interruptedly pale at suture, lateral margins pale, a pale spot at their distal end, and a short transverse bar across clypeus at this level, genae with margins pale below antennae, and transversely pale at level of suture, antennae with second segment fuscous; pronotum fuscous, disk much paler, carinae pale testaceous, edged fuscous, mesonotum yellowish brown, fuscous anteriorly, median and lateral carinae pale testaceous, edged with fuscous, a pale crescentic spot on each side of median carina near middle, a round pale spot, incomplete, with a fuscous inner ring and a pale center, near base of each lateral carina mesially, a narrow transverse fuscous bar before scutellum, which is palely margined; tegmina semitransparent, dull yellowish brown, veins concolorous, bordered with transparent round spots, an interrupted series of pale areas between node and apex of clavus, apex of membrane submarginally fuscous, veins of membrane and apical margin pale; wings clouded smoky, veins darker.

Ovipositor with lateral styles broad, in profile both margins convex, the dorsal margin strongly so, curved downward distally to bluntly pointed apex with narrow apical membrane, styles curved mesad distally, a horizontal dorsal lobe directed posteriorly lying mesad and attached at base; second valvulae narrow, rodlike, converging distally; first valvulae ventrally with a thin membranous tapering process directed caudad, underlain by a sclerotized rounded lobe, about half as long as membrane and toothed minutely on apical border, dorsally a process sclerotized on upper margin which is decurved apically and bears three teeth three-quarters from base and two large spines distally.

Described from two females taken by the writer in St. John's Valley, Trinidad, B. W. I. (Aug. 10, 15, 1942), resting on low branches of shrubs. Type, U. S. N. M. No. 56703.

This genus is distinguished by the flat and prominently carinated vertex, by the venation of tegmina and wings, and by the shape of the lobes of the lateral styles of the ovipositor; the species is distinguished by its size and by the color pattern.

OPSIPLANON NEMOROSUS, new species

PLATE 14, FIGURES 377–384

Female: Length, 3.0 mm.; tegmen, 2.8 cm.

Vertex dark fuscous, median carina and lateral margins testaceous, a large pale oval spot on each side of middle line, frons, clypeus, genae and antennae fuscous, frons minutely speckled with testaceous spots in basal half, clypeus with a small testaceous spot on each side of middle line at suture, genae with a pale transverse line at this level, with a pale line from its inner end down posterior edge; pronotum fuscous, carinae pale, a pale spot on disk on each side of middle line; mesonotum fuscous, carinae pale, three testaceous spots on disk on each side of middle line, three pale spots on each side laterad of disk; tegmina fuscous, conspicuously marked with round pale transparent spots, veins fuscous, membrane smoky, veins paler, becoming pallid or white at apex; wings rather smoky, veins darker; profemora and mesofemora fuscous, suffused pale at base and apex, one or two pale spots dorsally, postfemora fuscous, protibiae and mesotibiae fuscous with a pale spot one-third from base, apical third pale, posttibiae fuscous with apical two-thirds paler on inner face, spines black, tarsal joints fuscous, pale apically, spines black; abdomen fuscous, membrane red.

Ovipositor with lateral styles subquadrate, ventral margin almost straight, dorsal margin convex near base, sharply decurved apically, apical margin truncate, sinuate, produced into a short blunt lobe at ventral angle, dorsally a thin horizontal lobe directed posteriorly lying mesad and attached at base; second valvulae narrow, sclerotized dorsally and ventrally at base, ventral margin produced into a shallow lobe apically; first valvulae ventrally with a thin bifid tapering lobe directed posteriorly, horizontal and underlain by a shorter sclerotized lobe obliquely truncate distally and minutely toothed, dorsal process of each valvula with upper margin decurved towards apex, with two small teeth subapically and a pair of larger curved spines at apex.

Described from one female taken by the writer in St. John's Valley, Trinidad, B. W. I. (July 20, 1942), resting on fiddlewood. This species is distinguished by its size and color pattern. Type, U.S.N.M. No. 56704.

Family TROPIDUCHIDAE

Subfamily TAMBINIINAE

10a. *Subcosta giving off several furcate veins to costal margin.*

Tribe ALCESTINI

Genus ALCESTIS Stål

Alcestis STÅL, Svenska Vet.-Akad. Handl., vol. 3, No. 6, p. 11, 1862. (Genotype, *Alcestis pallescens* Stål, *ibid.*)

Vertex broader than long in middle, lateral margins parallel, apex rounded, posterior margin shallowly excavate, median carina usually present; frons longer than wide (about 1.5:1), medially carinate, margins subparallel, more ampliate in distal third; clypeus rather small, lateral margins not carinate; antennae short. Pronotum as long as vertex, tricarinate, lateral carinae diverging posteriorly, anterior border arcuately convex, posterior border emarginate, sometimes with a median notch; mesonotum broader than long, tricarinate, lateral carinae arcuate, joined to median carina anteriorly. Tegmina broad, costal margin strongly curved, sutural margin straight or nearly so, oblique, subcosta and radius giving off several branches, usually furcate, to costal margin. Posttibiae with three spines.

ALCESTIS VITREA, new species

PLATE 14, FIGURES 385–389

Male: Length, 6.0 mm.; tegmen, 6.4 mm.   Female: Length, 6.4 mm.; tegmen, 7.0 mm.

Vertex broader than long in middle (2.4:1), median carina obsolete, frons longer than wide (1.4:1), median carina feebly present, rather broad. Tegmina with anterior vein (costa) reaching margin basad of middle, 13 oblique transverse veins attaining costal margin, $Sc+R$ forking one-quarter from base, Sc giving off four branches, two or three of them bifurcate anteriorly, R with four branches apically, M with six, Cu_1 with seven reaching margin, apex of clavus distad of middle.

Pallid green; transverse veinlets near margin of tegmen and a spot near commissural margin at junction of claval veins fuscous.

Anal segment of male three times as long as broad, bifid at apex, widened distad of anus which is somewhat before middle. Aedeagus with periandrium short, comprising a ring basally with its ventral margin produced posteriorly, the ventral prolongation troughlike, with an oblique lobe on each side apically, that on right side finger-like, the other twice as broad; penis tubular, upturned distally, a deeply bifurcate process arising on left near base, the dorsal limb sloping upward, then mesad across middle, then bent outward, the ventral limb with parallel sides, narrow, directed horizontally backward, sharply deflexed at apex where it is somewhat footlike in outline, distad of this process penis with two pointed flattened plates in middle apically, surrounded by a thick membrane.

Ovipositor with first valvulae narrow, elongate, bearing nine or ten small spines on distal half of dorsal margin, the apical pair larger than the others; lateral styles narrow, with eight or nine small teeth at apex, four large on apical margin, four or five small submarginally in an approximately parallel row.

Egg elongate-ovoid, with sides subparallel for most of their length, smooth, obliquely truncate at one pole with a minute process at apex, situated on a narrow hyaline rim, traversed by several wavy lines.

Described from eight males and nine females collected by the writer at Santa Margarita, Trinidad, B. W. I., on various dates in July and August 1942. This species is nearest to *A. surinamensis* Schmidt, from which it differs in the proportions of the vertex and in the venation of the costal area. Holotype male and allotype, U.S.N.M. No. 56705; paratype in B.M.N.H.

10*b*. *Subcosta not giving off furcate veins to costal margin, tegmina pellucid, with a line of transverse veins distad of middle.*

Tribe TAMBINIINI

ROESMA, new genus

Vertex much longer than broad, produced before eyes in a tapering process as long as pronotum and mesonotum combined, shallowly tectiform, slightly upturned distally, median carina narrowly furcate on basal third, simple on distal two-thirds, lateral margins parallel between eyes, gradually converging almost in a straight line distally, abruptly curved mesad at apex; frons much longer than broad, flattened, median carina distinct, lateral margins subparallel, slightly concave or sinuate basad of antennae, thence somewhat ampliate, curving inwardly to suture distally; clypeus short, with a weak median carina; rostrum scarcely reaching to mesocoxae; antennae with second segment three times as long as first, about three times as long as greatest width, expanding to apex, with sensoria in distal half. Pronotum about as long as eyes, convexly produced anteriorly, rather deeply emarginate posteriorly, disk tricarinate, two carinae on margin behind eye on each side; mesonotum tricarinate, lateral carinae meeting median carina anteriorly, scutellum transversely grooved at line of junction with disk. Hind tibiae with three spines. Tegmina with an extremely short Sc+R+M stalk, not exceeding one-third length of basal cell, Sc+R fork very close to nodal line, of cross veins, M forking about middle of tegmen, with a second fork on posterior branch before cross veins, Cu$_1$ forking between first M fork and union of claval veins, claval veins uniting one-third from base, apex of clavus nearly three-quarters from base of tegmen. Ovipositor with third valvulae armed with fourteen teeth on apical margin. Egg subcylindrical, rounded at one pole, obliquely truncate and operculate at other, opercular rim thickened, slightly expanded anteriorly, surmounted laterally with a vertical membranous collar, joined anteriorly to a short knoblike vertical chorionic process.

This genus differs from *Athestia* Melichar in the shape of the vertex and of the tegmina, and in venation, and from *Remosa* Distant in the shape of the vertex, in the posteriorly forked median carina, in the number of teeth on the third valvulae and in the shape of the egg.

Genotype: *Roesma grandis*, new species.

ROESMA GRANDIS, new species

PLATE 14, FIGURES 390-396

Female: Length, 11.3 mm.; tegmen, 8.6 mm.

Vertex in middle two and a quarter times as long as broad; frons longer than broad (3.2:1), shallowly tectiform from base to level of eyes, then flattened to apex, median carina distinct except near apex, where it is feeble, lateral carinae distad of level of eyes. Tegmina with Sc with two veins at apex, R with four, M with eight, Cu_{1a} with three, Cu_{1b} with two, costal cell devoid of transverse veins.

Pale green; eyes red, posttibial spines piceous at tip, a pale yellowish band along costal margin, genitalia fuscous in sclerotized parts.

Anal segment short, rather narrow, produced laterally distad of anus into rounded lobes. Ovipositor with lateral styles elongate, dorsal margin almost straight and horizontal, apical margin curved, obliquely truncate, ventral margin deeply excavated near base, an irregular row of five teeth at apex passing into a regular row of nine teeth along ventral margin; second valvulae thin, narrow, bladelike; first valvulae narrow, very slightly upturned, dorsal margin straight, or very slightly concave, ventral margin convex, a row of five small teeth on dorsal margin, two larger teeth directed obliquely upwards at apex, two small teeth on ventral margin below the former.

Egg subcylindrical, rounded at one pole, obliquely truncate with a thickened opercular rim, a thick rounded semitransparent membranous layer above it, with a minute chorionic process on uppermost edge; 1.2 mm. long, 0.36 mm. broad.

Described from one female taken by the writer in St. John's Valley, Trinidad, B. W. I. (Aug. 18, 1942). Type, U.S.N.M. No. 56706.

Family NOGODINIDAE

Genus NOGODINA Stål

Nogodina STÅL, Svenska Vet.-Akad. Handl., vol. 3, No. 6, p. 70, 1862. (Genotype, *Flata reticulata* Fabricus, designated by Schmidt, Ent. Zeit. Stettin, vol. 80, p. 157, 1919.)

Frons longer than broad, lateral margins parallel to level of antennae, then curved mesad to suture, lateral margins slightly elevated, median carina present, lateral carinae present or absent; clypeus tricarinate; vertex short, fully three times as broad as long, anterior margin transverse, posterior margin broadly excavated. Pronotum short, slightly longer than vertex along middle line; mesonotum with lateral carinae present, median carina obsolete. Posttibiae with three spines. Tegmina large, hyaline, costal membrane traversed by numerous cross veins, costal margin slightly curved, Sc, R, M, and Cu_1 arising separately from basal cell, nodal line, apical line, and anterior half of subapical line of cross veins present.

NOGODINA RETICULATA (Fabricius)

PLATE 14, FIGURES 414–418

Flata reticulata FABRICIUS, Systema rhyngotorum, p. 47, 1803.

Female: Length, 6.2 mm.; tegmen, 7.8 mm.

.Vèrtex with anterior margin straight, flattened; frons with median carina present, lateral carinae obsolete.

Fuscous; tegmina with costal membrane infuscate, with three hyaline spots, apical margin broadly infuscate, a narrow interrupted fuscous band from costa to commissural margin at basal third, and a similar band along nodal line; wings infuscate at apical margin.

Ovipositor with lateral styles broad, dorsal margin horizontal, slightly curved upward distally, ventral margin excavate basally, apical margin rounded; second valvulae narrow, dorsal and ventral margins converging to middle, then slightly diverging, continuing subparallel to rounded apex; first valvulae narrow, dorsal margin straight, ventral margin slightly convex, a row of eight teeth dorsally on distal half, a narrow bladelike lobe attached on inner face basally, directed posteriorly.

Egg ovoid, 2.4 times longer than broad, smooth, not operculate.

Described from one female specimen taken by Dr. J. G. Myers in Surinam (May 29, 1929).

Genus BLADINA Stål

Bladina STÅL, Berliner Ent. Zeitschr., vol. 3, p. 324, 1859. (Genotype, *Bladina fuscovenosa* Stål.)

Head with eyes nearly as broad as pronotum; vertex short, about four times as broad as long in middle, lateral margins subparallel, anterior margin straight or very slightly curved, carinate, posterior margin broadly excavate; frons longer than broad, lateral margins nearly parallel to below level of antennae, then incurved to fronto-clypeal suture, median carina percurrent, lateral carinae absent, sometimes indicated basally, a row of pustules inside each lateral margin; clypeus tricarinate. Pronotum twice as long as vertex in middle, anterior margin convex, posterior margin broadly excavate, median carina present; mesonotum tricarinate, lateral carinae straight, sometimes meeting a curved transverse ridge anteriorly. Posttibiae with four spines. Tegmina with costal and commissural margins parallel, not diverging apically, costal membrane narrow, traversed by irregular veinlets, Sc + R united basally in a common stalk, M branching in basal third, Cu_1 simple, membrane with many supernumerary longitudinal veins, with numerous irregular transverse veinlets between them, usually no distinct transverse line on membrane or at most an irregular line.

BLADINA FUSCOVENOSA Stål

PLATE 14, FIGURES 397-399

Bladina fuscovenosa STÅL, Berliner Ent. Zeitschr., vol. 3, p. 324, 1859.

Male: Length, 5.0 mm.; tegmen, 7.2 mm.

Frons with lateral margins scarcely diverging to below level of antennae, median carina distinct, a row of pustules near lateral margin on each side.

Yellowish brown; posttibiae lined fuscous; tegmina very pale, transparent, veins brown, transverse veinlets on corium pale, wings hyaline, slightly clouded brown, veins brown; eyes sometimes barred with crescentic dark purplish bands.

Anal segment narrow, strongly deflexed ventrally distad of anus, telson long. Aedeagus complex, periandrium with a vertical, thin, tapering process medially on dorsal margin, with a short strutlike ridge transversely on each side at its base, a pair of long narrow flattened processes, directed vertically, arising ventrally at apex, each abruptly narrowed subapically into a slender point which is bent mesad; penis with a pair of long simple slender spines at apex, directed vertically. Genital styles broad, dorsal margin straight, with a slight elevation before apex, ventral margin distinctly convex, apical margin obliquely truncate.

Described from one male collected by Dr. J. G. Myers at San Fernando de Apure, Venezuela (Dec. 31, 1930). Specimen deposited in B.M.N.H.

BLADINA FUSCANA Stål

PLATE 14, FIGURES 400-405

Bladina fuscana STÅL, Svenska Vet.-Akad. Handl., vol. 3, No. 6, p. 13, 1862.

Male: Length, 5.4 mm.; tegmen, 7.8 mm. Female: Length, 5.4 mm.; tegmen, 7.9 mm.

Dark fuscous; tegmina somewhat darker along costal membrane, transverse veinlets dark, conspicuous, wings hyaline, bordered fuscous at hind margin, veins brown.

Anal segment strongly deflexed posteriorly distad of anus, telson long. Aedeagus complex, periandrium broad, ventral border strongly convex, curved upward distally, a laterally compressed tapering process in middle of dorsal margin directed vertically, distad of this a smaller and narrower vertical process, also medial, on each side at apex of dorsal margin a thin vertical lobe, rounded at tip, slightly curved anteriorly, a median spine ventrally at apex; penis tubular basally, bifid near apex, each lobe terminating in a long curved spine directed upward, lobes at base of these spines beset with numerous small teeth directed upward, the teeth of the upper inner margin of each lobe, about eleven in number, much longer than the remainder, the most dorsal tooth bifurcate, a pair of curved spines ventrally, attached near middle line distally, each spine with a semicircular excavation at basal third on one margin with a short curved spine at the same level on other margin.   Genital styles broad, with sides strongly curved, dorsal margin straight, upturned near apex, ventral margin slightly convex, upturned distally, apical angle obliquely truncate as seen in profile.

Described from six males and eight females collected by the writer on pineapple (February 1936), on *Bromelia pinguin* (April 1941), and on *Rhoeo discolor* (May 25, June 7, 1942) at St. Augustine, and in the Botanic Gardens, Port of Spain, Trinidad, B. W. I.   Material in B.M.N.H.

BLADINA RUDIS (Walker)

PLATE 14, FIGURES 406–413

Flatoides rudis WALKER, List of specimens of homopterous insects in the collection of the British Museum, vol. 2, p. 421, 1851.

Male: Length, 6.0 mm., tegmen, 7.0 mm.

Frons with a series of rather transversely linear pustules inside each lateral margin; median carina distinct on vertex, posterior half of pronotum and on mesonotum; posttibiae with four spines, the basal spine minute.

Dark testaceous; eyes dark gray banded with fuscous arcs, ocelli bordered red, pronotum mostly pale, dark testaceous near anterior margin of disk and narrowly along posterior margin, with approximately 15 fuscous dots on each side, arranged in two rows, the first submarginal anteriorly, mesonotum fuscous, slightly paler on disk; tegmina fuscous between Sc and costal margin, and in posterior half of clavus, with an irregular reticulum of pale veinlets, corium otherwise testaceous-transparent, membrane more distinctly brown, vein R testaceous, remainder of veins on corium brown, a small fuscous spot on M at basal fork, a similar spot on Cu near basal cell, veins of membrane fuscous; wings transparent, somewhat clouded pale fuscous distally, veins brown.

Anal segment strongly deflexed distad of anus, telson long. Aedeagus complex; a laterally compressed broad tapering median process at middle of dorsal border, directed vertically, distad of this, on each side of aedeagus dorsally a pair of slender vertical spines, with their tips curved anteriorly, between the posterior of these and the apex a pair of slender vertical processes on each side, half as long as the anterior pair, the basad of this pair furcate, the distad simple; a curved, elongate, spinose process loosely attached near apex, giving off two parallel shorter spines at right angles about middle.   Genital styles broad, dorsal margin almost straight, ventral margin strongly convex, truncate dorsoapically with a slight projection at dorsal angle.

Described from one male collected by D. Farrell, St. Augustine, Trinidad, B. W. I. (1920). Material in B. M. N. H. This species is distinguished by the venation of the tegmina and wings, by the structure of the aedeagus, and by the color.

Genus BIOLLEYANA Distant

Biolleyana DISTANT, Ann. Mag. Nat. Hist., ser. 8, vol. 4, p. 335, 1909.   (Genotype, *Nogodina pictifrons* Stål, Ent. Zeit. Stettin, vol. 25, pp. 53, 369, 1864.)

Head with eyes about as broad as pronotum, vertex short, more than twice as broad as long, lateral margins parallel, raised, anterior margin carinate, angulately produced anteriorly, posterior margin roundly excavate; frons longer than broad, lateral margins almost parallel, diverging very slightly from base to apical three-quarters, then incurved to frontoclypeal suture, slightly raised, median carina distinct, lateral carinae feeble; clypeus tricarinate.   Pronotum with anterior margin strongly convex, posterior margin broadly excavated; mesonotum with median carina distinct, lateral carinae present, curved mesad basally, subparallel along sides of disk, then curved mesad anteriorly to meet rather acutely at middle line.   Posttibiae with four or five spines.   Tegmina rather broad, expanding distally, vitreous, veins prominent, a series of transverse veins between costa and margin, Sc and R with a common basal stalk longer than basal cell, M fork, fork of Cu_1 and junction of claval veins at about same level, nodal line, subapical line and apical line of transverse veins present, a transverse vein in clavus between claval suture and anterior claval vein at basal third.   Wings with a fairly even line of subapical areoles and an evener row at apical margin.

BIOLLEYANA COSTALIS (Fowler)

PLATE 14, FIGURES 419–422; PLATE 15, FIGURES 423–432

Sassula costalis FOWLER, Biologia Centrali-Americana, Rhynch. Hom., vol. 1, p. 68, 1900.

Male: Length, 8.2 mm.; tegmen, 10.7 mm.   Female: Length, 8.5 mm.; tegmen, 11.5 mm.

Vertex about three times as broad across base as long in middle; frons about one and a half times as long as wide, lateral carinae obsolete on apical third.

Fuscous, abdomen and legs paler; tegmina hyaline, usually a spot on costal membrane at basal third, a spot at basal $M-Cu_1$ cross vein, a short line from stigma along nodal line to M, and three or four diffuse patches distad of subapical line dark fuscous; wings with apical cells infuscate except for a clear spot in M.

Anal segment of male in profile expanding distally, deflexed beyond anus, dorsal margin almost straight, ventral margin sinuately convex, apex truncate, with a median channel to anal foramen. Aedeagus tubular, bent into a U shape, comprising dorsally a thin flat membrane concave at apex, its sides strongly deflexed and tapering to apical angles where they are produced into a point; below this membrane a pair of processes on each side, the outer in the form of a slender tapering rod, pointed at apex, the inner similarly curved, broader, rounded at apex, with a slender filament arising subapically on its ventral margin, enclosing a U-shaped hollow; ventrally a pair of processes on each side, the inner long, bladelike, semimembranous, tapering gradually to apex, the outer small, less than half length of preceding, sinuate, with the pointed apex directed dorsally. Genital styles fairly broad, dorsal and ventral margins convex, apical process vertical, somewhat peglike, slightly curved anteriorly, truncate at apex.

Anal segment of female short, in profile obliquely truncate distally, rather deflexed beyond anus, lateral angles not produced. Ovipositor with lateral styles broad, dorsal margin straight, ventral margin convex, curving strongly upward distally, devoid of an apical process; first valvulae elongate, narrow, dorsal margin straight with three single teeth, widely spaced, and distad of them two alternated rows of about three teeth each, apex pointed with a single tooth below it, ventral margin shallowly convex; a thinner lobe of same size as preceding adpressed against its inner face, attached at base.

Egg elongate-ovate, narrower at one pole, with a slight impression laterally near the more rounded pole, smooth, 1.2 mm. long, 0.5 mm. wide.

Described from one male and four females collected by W. Buthn at Hacienda Tenguel, Ecuador (Aug. 20, 1920), labeled "abundant on cacao."

Genus VARCIOPSIS Jacobi

Varciopsis JACOBI, Deutsche Ent. Zeitschr., 1915, p. 312. (Genotype, *Ricania trigutta* Walker, List of specimens of homopterous insects in the collection of the British Museum, Suppl., p. 104, 1858.)

Vertex short, more than four times as broad as long in middle, anterior border transverse, slightly angulately produced, carinate, lateral margins subparallel, strongly raised, posterior margin rather deeply roundingly excavate, median carina obsolete; frons longer than broad, flat, lateral margins raised, subparallel, scarcely diverging to level of antennae then curved inward to frontoclypeal suture, median carina distinct, obsolete in apical seventh, lateral carinae distinct on basal half, obsolete on apical half; clypeus tricarinate; antennae with first segment very short, second segment cylindrical, slightly expanded distally. Pronotum in middle at least one and a half times as long as vertex on same line, anterior margin strongly convexly produced, posterior margin angularly excavate, median carina distinct, lateral carinae diverging parallel with hind margin of eyes; mesonotum with disk flat, tricarinate, carinae united anteriorly. Posttibiae with four spines. Tegmina with costal margin markedly rounded, costal membrane ample, Sc and R with a common stalk basally, M forking about level with union of claval veins, Cu_1 forking at same level or slightly more distad, nodal line, subapical line and apical line of transverse veins present, claval veins united about middle of clavus, anterior vein not connected with claval suture by a transverse vein, two or three transverse veins near apex of clavus.

VARCIOPSIS TENGUELANA, new species

PLATE 15, FIGURES 433–440

Male: Length, 8.5 mm.; tegmen, 11.0 mm.

Vertex about 4.5 times as broad as long in middle; frons 1.3 times longer than broad.

Testaceous or pale brown, carinae of mesonotum fuscous, legs testaceous, abdomen brown, tinged red at hind border of each segment; tegmina hyaline, veins brown, fuscous spot at stigma extending narrowly posteriorly to a round spot adjoining nodal line at R, apical areoles clouded brown near margin with a distinctly larger dark area in two or three apical areoles in M; wings hyaline, apical areoles clouded brown in distal quarter.

Anal segment of male narrow in profile, deflexed beyond arms, truncate at apex, apical lateral angles slightly pointed. Aedeagus tubular, a pair of broad, rather shallowly curved lobes ventrally tapering to a slender point distally, ventrolaterad, halfway from base of aedeagus, a short flattened distally sinuate spine directed posteriorly on each side, laterally on each side of aedeagus a thin simple spine, directed posteriorly, above this a long sclerotized rod, bifurcate distally and slightly curved mesad, attaining apex of aedeagus. Genital styles broad, dorsal margin in profile almost straight, ventral margin slightly convex, apical margin slightly sinuate, apical process long, peglike, directed upward and slightly curved anteriorly, truncate at apex.

Described from two males collected by W. Buthn on cacao at Hacienda Tenguel, Ecuador (Aug. 20, 1920). Type in B.M.N.H.; paratype, U.S.N.M. No. 56707. According to W. E. China, who compared this species with Walker's type of *Ricania trigutta*, it differs from the type in tegminal venation and genitalia. *V. trigutta* has a half line of transverse veins between the subapical line and the transverse fold; the color pattern is the same in both species.

Family FLATIDAE

11a. Tegmina steeply tectiform.

Subfamily FLATINAE

12a. Tegmina broadly rounded apically, area distad of apex of clavus not very large, costal cell about twice width of costal membrane.

Tribe FLATINI

Genus POEKILLOPTERA Latreille

Poekilloptera LATREILLE, Précis des caractères génériques des insectes . . ., Hémiptères, p. 90, 1796. (Genotype, *Cicada phalaenoides* Linnaeus, designated by Latreille, Histoire naturelle . . ., Cicadaires, vol. 12, p. 315, 1804.)

Vertex very short, anterior margin transverse, carinate; frons with lateral margins arcuate, slightly raised, median carina present in part; pronotum short, anteriorly convex, elongate laterad and carinate; mesonotum inflated. Tegmina large, costal and apical margins broadly rounded, costal cell short, broader than costal membrane. Posttibiae unispinose.

POEKILLOPTERA PHALAENOIDES (Linnaeus)

PLATE 15, FIGURE 473; PLATE 16, FIGURE 474

Cicada phalaenoides LINNAEUS, Systema naturae, ed. 10, vol. 1, p. 438, 1758.— JACOBI, Sitzb. Ges. Nat. Freunde Berlin, 1904, p. 9.

Head, thorax, legs, costal margin at base, and anal segment of female yellowish orange, heavily powdered white in life; tegmina pale, with round black spots, chiefly in basal half.

Anal segment of male rather short, apical margin truncate or shallowly indented at middle, apical angles rounded, anus situated at basal third, segment in profile very slightly decurved. Pygofer broad, lateral margins slightly curved, ventral margin sinuate, indented medially. Aedeagus with periandrium tubular, deeply cleft laterally at apex, median ventral process narrowing distally and passing into a sclerotized point, dorsal margin broad, truncate at apex; penis tubular, bifid in apical half, each limb curved upward distally into a spine, half as long as aedeagus, directed anteriorly above periandrium. Genital styles broad, expanding gradually apically, apical margin oblique, apical process a vertical spine, slightly curved anteriorly.

Anal segment of female large, broader than long, slightly tectiform, broadly rounded at margin, anus situated two-thirds from base. Ovipositor with lateral styles broad, thick, with a single even line of nine teeth on posterior margin directed mesad; second valvulae apposed medially, semimembranous, ventral margin very slightly convex, dorsal margin sinuate, a minute fleshy reflexed process, rather spatulate in shape, basally on ventral surface; first valvulae broad, somewhat twisted at base, convex on both margins on basal two-thirds, then tapering with straight sides to a point, a small thin tapering lobe attached to inner face of each near base.

Egg ovoid, obliquely compressed on one side, with a narrow opercular surface not quite two-thirds length of egg; a series of about six shallow longitudinal grooves spaced across two-thirds of circumference. Length, 1.3 mm.; breadth, 0.6 mm.

The Trinidad form has the tegmen rather heavily speckled in two bands, one with about 44 spots in anterior half of tegmen between costa and media, the other with about 21 spots on each side of Cu_1 and between suture and anterior claval vein (var. *phalaenoides*). Numerous specimens are at hand collected during 1942 at St. Augustine, Trinidad, B. W. I., by the writer.

12b. *Tegmina truncate apically or narrowed in distal half.*

13a. *Tegmina not narrowed distally, apical margin truncate or very shallowly rounded.*

14a. *Tegmina much expanded distally, sutural angle produced, more or less acute.*

Tribe FLATISSINI

Genus CARTHAEOMORPHA Melichar

Carthaeomorpha MELICHAR, Ann. Nat. Hofmus. Wien, vol. 16, p. 198, 1901. (Genotype, *Carthaeomorpha rufipes* Melichar, designated by Oshanin, Katalog der paläarktischen Hemipteren, p. 125, 1912.)

Vertex short, about four times as broad as long in middle, lateral margins diverging anteriorly, anterior margin carinate, somewhat produced, posterior margin broadly excavate; frons as broad as long or longer, flattened, lateral margins slightly arcuate, incurved below level of antennae, median carina present basally, obsolete distally, lateral carinae present at base. Pronotum short, about twice as long as vertex, anterior margin convexly produced, posterior margin broadly excavated; mesonotum with disk almost flat. Posttibiae with two spines in distal half. Tegmina large, subtriangular, costal margin not ampliately rounded, apex truncate, sutural angle acutely pointed, costal margin narrower than costal cell, Sc simple to apex, R forking about middle, M and Cu_1 forking in basal third, M fork slightly basad of Cu_1 fork.

CARTHAEOMORPHA BREVICEPS Melichar

PLATE 15, FIGURES 441–446

Carthaeomorpha breviceps MELICHAR, Ann. Nat. Hofmus. Wien, vol. 17, p. 34, 1902.

Female: Length, 10 mm.; tegmen, 12 mm.

Yellowish green; costal margin of tegmina narrowly pale, apical margin narrowly bordered red, apical cells distally very pale fuscous, transverse veins of whole tegmen orange, the membranous areas between them with minute orange specks, wings milk white, veins at base pink, apex of anal segment of female pink, protibiae and mesotibiae reddish. Insect powdered very pale green.

Anal segment of female short, in dorsal view ovate, broad at base, tapering toward apex, apex rounded with a median notch, distal portion shallowly channeled, telson arising distad of middle. Ovipositor with lateral styles large, subtriangular, sinuate on dorsal margin, lower margin curved with a row of 21 teeth, in a single row distally, in pairs basally; second valvulae laterally compressed, with lower margin straight, an asymmetrical excavation at apex, dorsal margin convex at base, sinuately narrowing to apex; first valvulae broad basally, tapering to apex, dorsal margin slightly convex with ten small teeth, a submarginal ridge passing to apex bearing eight small teeth in basal two-thirds and five larger teeth distally, a thin tapering lobe, with minutely shagreen surface, adpressed on inner face, attached at base.

Egg approximately ovoid, obliquely truncate at one pole, with a short crease extending for one-quarter length of egg, bordered on each side by a thickening of the shell, reticulately patterned and traversed by numerous fine parallel lines; length, 1.0 mm., width, 0.4 mm.

Described from one female collected by F. W. Urich (1920), no locality being given. Melichar gives "Sudamerika, Brasilien, Bahia" as the locality for his material, and until confirmed Urich's specimen must be considered a doubtful Trinidad record.

14b. *Tegmina not much expanded distally, sutural angle not produced, or if so rounded, not acutely pointed.*

Tribe NEPHESINI

Genus EPORMENIS, new name

Ormenis METCALF, Bull. Mus. Comp. Zool., vol. 82, p. 394, 1938 (not *Ormenis* Stål, 1862). (Genotype, *Poeciloptera roscida* Germar by present designation.)

Vertex very short; frons as broad as long or broader, median carina present only on basal half, lateral margins curved; clypeus devoid of carinae. Pronotum convex anteriorly, concave posteriorly, smooth, with a small impression on each side of middle line; mesonotum devoid of carinae, or with median carina scarcely indicated at base or apex and lateral carinae at base. Hind tibiae with two spines before apex. Tegmina with anterior and posterior margins subparallel, costal margin not ampliate, costal membrane generally wider than costal cell, Sc strong, simple to apex, R forking about one-third from base, M forking level with R fork or slightly basad, Cu_1 forking rather basad of M fork, base of R and M granulate, apical and subapical lines of transverse veins even and distinct, a few irregular cross veins between node and apex of clavus, apical veins forked or simple in irregular sequence.

EPORMENIS ARIPENSIS, new species

PLATE 15, FIGURES 447-454

Male: Length, 6.0 mm.; tegmen, 6.3 mm. Female: Length, 5.7 mm.; tegmen, 6.3 mm.

Frons broader than long (1.4:1). Tegmina with costal membrane 1.8 times as wide as costal cell at level of R fork, apical areoles short, two-thirds length of subapical areoles, apical margin rounded, slightly oblique, apical angle more broadly rounded than sutural angle.

Pale green; dorsal surface of second antennal joint, tibial and tarsal spines black. Insect in life powdered greenish white.

Anal segment of male with apical portion deflexed through 45°, slightly longer than basal portion, a small broad lobe medioventrally at base. Aedeagus tubular, curved upward distally, with a pair of stout spines of half its length arising from middle line ventrally near apex, diverging and directed anteriorly. Genital styles broad, dorsal margin straight, ventral margin convex, upturned distally, apical process in form of a broad tooth tapering rather rapidly to an incurved point.

Anal segment of female short, rather broad, deflexed at apex. Ovipositor with lateral styles broad, thick, with stout teeth on posterior margin in two irregular rows; first valvulae with four blunt teeth apically.

Egg ovoid, distinctly compressed laterally, truncate obliquely at one pole, slightly crescentic in profile, with a long groove extending for three-quarters of length from one pole, with greatly thickened margins, minutely canaliculate; a pair of shallow longitudinal depressions weakly present on opposite side of egg; length, 0.9 mm., width, 0.3 mm.

Described from one male and one female taken in forest on Aripo, Northern Range, Trinidad, B. W. I., by Dr. J. G. Myers (Nov. 29, 1930), and one male and female taken by the writer on *Cordia* sp., St. John's Valley, Trinidad (Aug. 20, 1942). Holotype male, U. S. N. M. No. 56708; allotype female in B.M.N.H. This species differs from *O. unimaculata* Fennah in the venation of the tegmina, in the shape of the genitalia, in the absence of a black spot at the apex of the clavus, and in the presence of one on the antennae. It is possibly conspecific with *O. albula* Walker, but as the type of *albula* has the abdomen missing the relationship cannot be settled with certainty.

EPORMENIS UNIMACULATA (Fennah)

PLATE 15, FIGURE 464

Ormenis unimaculata FENNAH, Proc. Ent. Soc. Washington, vol. 43, p. 209, pl. 21, figs. 27, 28, 1941.

The anal segment of this species is asymmetrically cleft or deeply emarginate laterally near apex, and the aedeagus also is markedly asymmetrical. Mr. China finds this very distinct from *O. nigrolimbata* Fowler in color pattern, size, structure of frons, and other details. The type of the latter is a female.

One male and one female collected by the writer on cacao, Santa Margarita, Trinidad, B. W. I. (July 16, 21, 1942), in addition to earlier records.

EPORMENIS FULIGINOSA (Fennah)

PLATE 16, FIGURES 476–478

Ormenis fuliginosa FENNAH, Proc. Ent. Soc. Washington, vol. 43, p. 204, pl. 21, figs. 23, 24, 1941.

The following data, based on a study of more material, will serve to amplify the original description of this species:

Angle between costal margin and middle of apical margin of tegmina 67°, angle between middle of apical margin and commissural margin 95°.

Anal segment of male of same length as aedeagus, apex remote from lower apical angle of genital styles, convex dorsally, scarcely deflexed distad of anus, not channeled distally in middle line, apical margin truncate, slightly sinuate, telson arising halfway between base and apex; ventral margin of segment in profile convex, rather shallowly curved.

Aedeagus with periandrium tubular, dorsal surface flattened, widened distally, obtusely angulate at apex, forming dorsal tip of aedeagus, a deep cleft laterally at apex, ventral surface narrowed distally into a vertical keel, pointed at apex; penis tubular, with a pair of spines on each side arising ventrally near apex, the shorter spines of each side of equal length, three-tenths as long as aedeagus (not one-sixth as previously given), the longer spines arising from a common base with the shorter and lying exterior to them, spine of left side very long and slender, nearly as long as aedeagus, spine of right side about half this length, shallowly curved. Genital styles with upper margin folded inward, expanded into a lobe in apical third.

Egg approximately ovoid, smooth, in front view with sides straight, narrowing slightly to one pole, one pole broadly rounded, the other bluntly angulate, one end of egg obliquely truncate in side view, a longitudinal groove for three-quarters of length, with margins thickened, a pair of shallow depressions, longitudinal and slightly curved, on opposite side of egg; length, 1.1 mm., width, 0.3 mm.

These additional data are based on four males and seven females taken by the writer on coffee and *Cordia* sp. at St. Augustine, Trinidad, B. W. I. (May 26 and Nov. 8, 1942).

Genus FLATORMENIS Melichar

Flatormenis MELICHAR, Genera insectorum, fasc. 182, p. 71, 1923. (Genotype, *Ormenis* ‌*quamulosa* Fowler.)

Frons broader than long, lateral margins strongly curved, median carina present only in basal half; tegmina with apical and nodal line present, the former about equidistant between latter and apical margin; costal membrane distad of humeral elevation much broader than costal cell; several but not most of the veins distad of apical line forked. Hind tibiae with two spines. Anal segment of male only slightly deflexed in side view, ventrolateral margins convex, a shallow groove between anus and apex dorsally.

FLATORMENIS SQUAMULOSA (Fowler)

PLATE 15, FIGURES 455–463

Ormenis squamulosa FOWLER, Biologia Centrali-Americana, Rhynch. Hom., vol. 1, p. 57, 1900.

Male: Length, 6.0 mm.; tegmen, 6.2 mm. Female: Length, 6.0 mm.; tegmen, 7.0 mm.

Frons broader than long in middle (1.4:1), median carina present only on basal half. Tegmina with costal membrane twice as wide as costal cell at level of R fork, an impressed fold basad of subapical line.

Head, pronotum, pleurites, and legs pale yellow, sometimes clouded fuscous, mesonotum reddish brown, darker laterally, abdominal sclerites fuscous, membrane pallid or yellow, genitalia fuscous; tegmina piceous or very dark fuscous, costal margin, and sometimes area between costal veinlets, and scutellar margin of clavus narrowly pale yellow, Sc testaceous; wings smoky, veins darker. Insect in life powdered pinkish brown and gray, rather speckled.

Anal segment of male short and broad, not deflexed markedly in apical half, ventral margin in profile convex, apex bluntly rounded, telson arising basad of middle. Aedeagus with periandrium tubular, slightly upturned distally; a thin rounded lobe on each side of middle line apically, a short stout spine laterad of each directed anteriorly with a row of about eleven minute recurved teeth laterally near base; lateral margins cleft at apex; a pair of stout shallowly curved spines, three-quarters length of aedeagus, arising distally and directed forward ventrolaterally; ventral surface of periandrium tapering distally to an upturned point; basad of this point, ventrolaterally, a slight ridge on each side bearing about eight recurved teeth; penis a simple tube slightly upturned distally, apically bifid, the cleft extending for one-seventh from apex, each limb expanded distally, curved dorsally and anteriorly, scroll-like. Genital styles broad, expanding distally, dorsal margin slightly convex, apical margin rounded, somewhat oblique, apical process a vertical spine, curving slightly anteriorly.

Anal segment of female short, broad, rounded at apex and scarcely deflexed. Ovipositor with lateral styles thick, broad, with a double row of seventeen strong teeth directed mesad on distal margin and a single tooth situated slightly basad on inner surface at dorsal end of row; second valvulae in profile tapering to a point, lower margin straight, oblique, upper margin straight with a round knob laterally halfway from base; medially in distal half a thin, vertical, broadly triangular plate with apex curved posteriorly; first valvulae broad, twisted at base, narrowed sharply to a point at apex, flanked on each side with a pair of short teeth; a thin tapering process attached mesally at base, directed posteriorly and adpressed to inner face of valvulae.

Egg ovoid, in anterior view slightly more narrowed toward one pole, in side view crescentic, obliquely truncate at one end, a longitudinal groove present for four-fifths of length, with its margins broadly thickened, traversed by numerous fine parallel lines; length, 0.9 mm.; width in side view, 0.45 mm.

Described from 24 males and 29 females taken by the writer at St. Augustine, Trinidad, B. W. I., on Liberian coffee and *Cordia* sp., *Lantana camara*, and *Hibiscus* between June 1942 and March 1943. This species is superficially similar to *Epormenis cestri* (Berg) but differs in color and in its smaller size.

Genus ORMENIS Stål

Ormenis STÅL, Svenska Vet.-Akad. Handl. vol. 3, no. 6, p. 68, 1862. (Genotype, *Poeciloptera perfecta* Walker, List of specimens of homopterous insects in the British Museum, vol. 2, p. 449, 1851 (=*Ormenis rufo-terminata* Stål), designated by Distant, Ann. Mag. Nat. Hist., ser. 8, vol. 5, p. 313, 1910.)
Ricanoyata MELICHAR, Genera insectorum, fasc. 182, p. 67, 1923.

Vertex short; frons as broad as long or broader, lateral margins arcuate, raised, a median carina present basally, clypeus ecarinate. Pronotum anteriorly convex, produced, posteriorly concave; mesonotum inflated, carinae obsolete. Tegmina subtriangular, markedly expanded distally, apical angle rounded, sutural angle rectangular, not produced, rounded at tip, costal membrane expanding distally, wider than costal cell; subapical line of transverse veins undulate, apical line parallel to apical margin, both incurved to reach costa anteriorly; clavus granulate. Wings larger than tegmina. Posttibiae bispinose.

ORMENIS ANTONIAE Melichar

PLATE 16, FIGURE 475

Ormenis antoniae MELICHAR, Ann. Nat. Hofmus. Wien, vol. 17, p. 94, pl. 5, fig. 11, 1902.
Ormenis rufa FENNAH, Proc. Ent. Soc. Washington, vol. 43, p. 206, 1941.

The following data are given to amplify the original description:

Ovipositor with lateral styles bearing 17 spines on apical margin in two rows, alternately arranged and directed mesad; second valvulae adpressed, with ventral surface slightly curved in profile, apex bluntly pointed, dorsal margin with a rounded eminence at base and a vertical sabot-shaped or clog-shaped lobe at middle, directed anteriorly and upward; first valvulae twisted at base, broad, tapering upward to a point at apex with two small teeth subapically on each margin, and a small rather isolated tooth basad of pair on dorsal margin, a thin semicrescentic lobe, with a thickened ridge attached at base of each valvula and adpressed to its inner face.

Five males and eight females, mostly of the pale form of this species, are to hand taken by the writer on Liberian coffee and mango at St. Augustine, Trinidad, B. W. I. (July 15, Sept. 29, 1942).

13b. *Tegmina narrowed distally, costal and apical margins sinuate.*

Tribe SELIZINI

LOCRONA, new genus

Vertex short, frons distinctly wider than long, lateral margins elevated, strongly incurved below level of antennae, median carina present in basal half, frontoclypeal suture impressed. Pronotum fully three times as long as vertex, smooth, devoid of carinae, anterior margin convex, posterior margin shallowly concave; mesonotum inflated anteriorly, carinae obsolete. Tegmina with margins expanding distally, costal margin not ampliately rounded, apical angle strongly curved, apical margin truncate, sutural angle markedly produced, rounded at tip, not acutely pointed, costal membrane much wider throughout than widest part of costal cell, Sc simple, joining costa at middle of tegmen, R forking basad of this point, M forking at about same level, Cu_1 forking basad of M fork, base of R and M, and posterior half of clavus granulate, apical line of transverse veins slightly irregular, distinct, subparallel to apical margin, subapical line fairly even, distinct and undulate, both lines meeting costa anteriorly, subapical and apical areoles of about equal length, apical veins mainly forked.

Anal segment of male with lower margin scarcely decurved, in dorsal view rounded at apex, shallowly channeled medially distad of anus, telson arising two-fifths from base.

Anal segment of female broadly ovate, rather longer than broad, apical margin roundly truncate, deflexed abruptly, with a short median channel distad of anus, telson arising at basal third. Ovipositor with lateral styles stout with about 20 teeth in two rows inside apical margin directed mesad.

This genus is apparently near *Leptodàscalia* Melichar but differs in the frontal proportions, the proportionately much wider costal membrane, and the shape of the sutural angle of the tegmina.

Genotype: *Ormenis nigrospersa* Fennah.

LOCRONA NIGROSPERSA (Fennah)

PLATE 15, FIGURES 470–472

Ormenis nigrospersa FENNAH, Proc. Ent. Soc. Washington, vol. 43, p. 205, pl. 21, figs. 29, 30, 1941.

The examination of further material makes it possible to amplify the original description with the following data:

Aedeagus with periandrium tubular, slightly curved upward distally, dorsal margin with a minutely toothed ridge on each side at base, bluntly pointed at apex, where it is slightly impressed, not quite reaching to tip of aedeagus, a short cleft on each side laterally, below which is a process curved backward, ventrad and then anteriorly, bifurcate about middle into two spines of unequal length, the longer about half as long as aedeagus; penis tubular, bifid for a short distance at apex, the middle portion at base of cleft pointed, the sclerotized apicolateral armature consisting of a minute vertical spine anteriorly, a scroll-like curved ledge ventrally, and a rather large lateral pouch.

Ovipositor with first valvulae tapering upward to a point, a pair of minute teeth on each side at its base, a thin lobe on inner face attached at base tapering distally; second valvulae with lower margin obliquely tapering upward, dorsal margin curved downward at base, then raised in a long transparent domelike elevation, distad of which it is sinuately decurved to apex.

Egg ovoid, surface delicately reticulate, a longitudinal groove extending for four-fifths length, bordered laterally with minute hairlike processes.

A series of six males and four females is at hand taken by the writer at Santa Margarita, Trinidad, B. W. I., on various dates between July and September 1942. The type is in the U. S. National Museum.

Genus ANADASCALIA Melichar

Anadascalia MELICHAR, Genera Insectorum, fasc. 182, p. 103, 1923. (Genotype, *Dascalia ornata* Melichar, Ann. Nat. Hofmus. Wien, vol. 17, p. 151, pl. 7, 1902.)

Vertex short, anterior margin straight or nearly so; frons a little longer than broad, lateral margins slightly curved and raised, median carina present only in basal half. Pronotum convex anteriorly, concave posteriorly, with an impression on each side of middle line; mesonotum inflated. devoid of carinae. Tegmina about twice as long as wide, the margins subparallel, apical margin truncate, apical angle widely rounded, sutural angle rectangular, not produced, an apical and a subapical line present, subparallel, the former not reaching to costa, apical veins short and simple, apical and subapical areoles of equal length, numerous transverse veins basad of subapical line. Posttibiae with two spines.

ANADASCALIA MERIDIONALIS, new species

PLATE 15, FIGURES 465–469

Female: Length, 8.0 mm.; tegmen, 9.1 mm.

Vertex short, a little more than half length of pronotum along middle line; width of head, with eyes, equal to width of thorax; frons as broad as long, lateral margins slightly curved, carinate, median carina present only in basal half, lateral carinae slightly indicated on tumescences at base; clypeus devoid of carinae. Pronotum convexly produced anteriorly, roundly excavated posteriorly, a median callus in anterior half with a depression on each side; mesonotum devoid of median carina, lateral carinae indicated in basal half. Hind tibiae with two spines. Tegmina 2.6 times longer than wide in middle, anterior and posterior margins subparallel; costal margin as wide as costal cell in middle, Sc simple to apex, reaching costa distad of apex of clavus, R forking about one-third from base, M forking slightly basad of R fork, Cu_1 forking basad of M fork, apical and subapical lines of transverse veins fairly even and distinct, a third row of areolets on inner side of subapical line, bounded basally by an irregular series of cross veins, basad of this cross veins numerous on corium. Wings with ten veins reaching apical margin before Cu_2.

Head pale testaceous, a small brown spot on vertex near each side anteriorly extending on to frons between base of lateral carinae and lateral margins, and on to anterodorsal angle of sides of head; pronotum pale testaceous, sparsely punctate with brown near anterior margin; mesonotum pale testaceous, a dark brown band around anterior margin of disk and extending two-thirds along its sides, a small dark spot inside each lateral carina at base; legs, abdomen, and genitalia pale testaceous. Tegmina translucent, pale, veins stramineous, irregularly sprinkled pale yellowish brown, darker in a distinct band from apical angle to middle of apical half of tegmen, apical and subapical lines outlined in yellowish brown, apical areolets yellowish brown to apex of clavus, interspersed with about seven hyaline rounded spots, each as wide as one apical areolet; clavus with transverse veins numerous and distinct, posterior claval vein narrowly fuscous; wings hyaline. Insect powdered pale buff.

Anal segment of female broadly rounded in dorsal view, only slightly deflexed apically. Ovipositor with lateral styles broad, narrowing towards apex, apical margin somewhat rounded with five stout incurved spines, a deflexed spine subapically near dorsal margin; second valvulae wedge-shaped in lateral view, narrowing posteriorly with a thin dorsal·cowl not quite overhanging apex; first valvulae narrow, rather flattened, upturned to a point apically, with four short longitudinal ridges, evenly spaced, each ending in a tooth on apical margin, the dorsal two ridges on each valvula with a few teeth subapically, a narrow wedge-shaped minutely setose process attached at base of valvula, adpressed to its inner face.

Described from two females collected by F. W. Urich in Trinidad, B. W. I. (1917). Type in British Museum mounted piecemeal on two microscope slides. Paratype, U. S. N. M. No. 57188. The quadrate vertex, the three series of areolets, the closely reticulate venation of the tegmina and the shape of the valvulae of the ovipositor readily distinguish this genus.

EUHYLOPTERA, new genus

Head with eyes about as wide as pronotum; vertex short, rounded into frons, apical margin in dorsal view slightly rounded, posterior margin shallowly concave, overlapped by pronotum; frons broader than long (about 1.2 to 1), flat basally, depressed near suture, median carina weakly present in basal half, absent in apical half, lateral carinae obsolete, lateral margins arcuate, not raised; clypeus devoid of carinae. Pronotum about as long as eyes, anteriorly convex, transverse in middle of margin, posterior margin angularly excavated, an impression on each side of middle line, a short ridge behind eyes; mesonotum with disk flattened, devoid of carinae. Hind tibiae with two spines before apex. Tegmina nearly 2.4 times as long as wide, costal margin strongly convex on basal two-thirds, thence slightly concave to apex, apical margin straight, obliquely truncate, forming an angle of 70° with the distal third of the costal margin, and one of 105° with the distal quarter of the commissural margin, apical margin nearly four-fifths as long as greatest width of tegmen; R forking at basal quarter, M forking just distad of R fork, Cu_1 forking slightly basad of R fork, apical line irregular but distinct, subapical line irregular, short. Wings about as long as tegmina.

Anal segment of male narrow, rather broader apically, deflexed in apical third, apical margin rounded, deeply notched, with a channel medially to anus, telson arising halfway from base.

Anal segment of female long, about as long as posttibiae, ovate, tectiform, anus subterminal. Ovipositor with lateral styles, small, subtriangular. Egg bluntly ovoid, smooth, not operculate.

This genus recalls *Cyarda* Walker but differs in the shape of the tegmina, which are relatively shorter, not so narrowed, and without a sinuate apical margin, and in the shape of the vertex, which is not produced anteriorly.

Genotype: *Euhyloptera corticalis*, new species.

EUHYLOPTERA CORTICALIS, new species

PLATE 16, FIGURES 479–486

Male: Length, 4.7 mm.; tegmen, 4.8 mm.   Female: Length, 5.0 mm.; tegmen, 5.1 mm.   Frons broader than long (1.2:1).

Testaceous or pale fuscous; genae and antennae pale yellow, mesonotum sometimes reddish brown, genitalia fuscous; tegmina brown, costal membrane, a line along Sc, R, M and Cu_1 about level of fork, a short band near apex of clavus, and membrane distad of node fuscous; veins pale testaceous; wings fuscous, veins dark.   Insect in life powdered dull brown.

Pygofer of male with anal angles of each side produced into a blunt lobe, lateral margins straight.   Genital styles broad, dorsal margin straight, excavated subapically, ventral margin strongly convex, apical process broad, truncate distally, with a minute point directed obliquely downward and backward.   Aedeagus tubular, curved upward distally, periandrium tubular, a serrate ridge on each side dorsolaterally at base, posterior dorsal margin pointed, posterior ventral margin broadly rounded; a long spinose process arising on each side near apex, curved ventrally and anteriorly, angularly bent at middle, and giving off at this point a slender filament directed posteriorly; penis broadly tubular, cleft at apex, with a short spine directed anteriorly and outward on each side of apex.

Egg 0.8 mm. long, 0.4 mm. wide, bluntly ovoid, not operculate.

Described from 9 males and 13 females taken by the writer at Santa Margarita, Trinidad, B. W. I., on various dates between May and December 1942 feeding on *Lantana camara*, *Cordia* sp., and low bushes.   Holotype male and allotype, U. S. N. M. No. 56709; paratype in B. M. N. H.

11b. Tegmina not steeply tectiform, nearly horizontal or gradually tectiform.

Subfamily FLATOIDINAE

Genus FLATOIDINUS Melichar

Flatoidinus MELICHAR, Genera insectorum, fasc. 182, p. 117, 1923. (Genotype, *Poeciloptera convivus* Stål, Svenska Vet.-Akad. Handl., vol. 3, No. 6, p. 13, 1862.)

Head with eyes narrower than the pronotum; vertex broader than long; frons rather longer than broad.   Pronotum about as long as vertex; mesonotum broader than long.   Tegmina with costal margin not undulate, about twice as long as broad, costal margin about twice as broad as costal cell, apical line distinct, subapical line present, irregular. Posttibiae bispinose.

FLATOIDINUS CORDIAE, new species

PLATE 16, FIGURES 487–492

Male: Length, 7.8 mm., tegmen, 8.0 mm. Female: Length, 9.2 mm.; tegmen, 10.5 mm.

Vertex broader than long (1.5:1); frons in middle slightly longer than broad (1.1:1), devoid of carinae, or lateral carinae scarcely indicated basally, lateral margins carinate; clypeus without carinae. Pronotum overlapping vertex anteriorly to a slight extent, as long as vertex; mesonotum with median carina indicated at base, lateral carinae basally present. Tegmina with costal area granulate, margin scarcely undulate, costal area fully twice as wide as costal cell, Sc simple to apex, R forking near middle of tegmina, M forking basad of R fork, Cu_1 forking still farther basad, base of R and M, R at fork and near nodal area granulate, apical line of cross veins uneven but distinct, subapical line parallel to apical margin, rather feebly indicated by irregular cross veins, clavus granulate near base.

Stramineous; vertex with a short black stripe on each side of middle line, subparallel to it or slightly oblique, frons slightly infuscate at base, genae with a small dark spot near ocellus, a black horizontal stripe before eye on each side, eyes red or gray, with concentric dark bands; pronotum with a black spot on each side of middle line, mesonotum testaceous with a dark spot on each side anteriorly, a dark spot on each side of middle line on disk, a pair of spots outside and a smaller pair inside lateral carinae at base; genitalia testaceous. Tegmina stramineous, costal area with about twelve spots occurring singly or in pairs, a spot or stripe on Sc one-third from base, a spot on M posterior to R fork, a larger spot at one-third and a linear spot at two-thirds from base on Cu_1, three small spots on M near subapical line, a spot at apex of Sc, a series of spots inside subapical areoles basally and apical areoles near margin, and a row of spots adjoining commissural margin in clavus fuscous or piceous; wings milk white, veins stramineous. Insect in life powdered grayish white.

Anal segment of male with posterior third only slightly deflexed, a large triangular median lobe ventrally. Aedeagus with two pairs of spinose processes at apex, the penial spines thick, directed anteriorly and obliquely upward for about half length of aedeagus, the periandrial spines slender, curved caudad from point of origin, then bending upward and forward in more than a semicircle, ventral margin of periandrium very deeply excavated, with each lateral prong pointed. Genital styles with dorsal and ventral margins parallel, apex obliquely truncate, apical process spinose, directed obliquely upward and caudad, then bent angularly obliquely cephalad.

Anal segment of female broadly ovate, rounded at apex. Ovipositor with lateral styles large and broad with about twelve teeth set in two rows on apical margin, directed mesad; second valvulae joined in middle line, ventral margin straight, dorsal margin steeply decurved from base, then more gradually tapering to pointed apex; first valvulae broad at base, tapering upward to apex, a few subapical teeth on each margin, a flat narrow tapering lobe on inner face attached at base.

Posterior margin of pregenital sternite with a short rectangular median excavation.

Egg ovoid, obliquely concave on two-thirds of one side, where the shell is thickened and minutely channeled, surface delicately reticulate; length, 1.0 mm.; width, 0.5 mm.

Described from one male and three females collected by the writer on black sage (*Cordia cylindrostachya*) and various shrubs (Nov. 3, 1936, April 4, 1941, Aug. 28, 1942) and one female collected by Miss B. L. Kerr from mango (July 14, 1943) at St. Augustine, Trinidad, B. W. I. Holotype male in B.M.N.H.; allotype, U.S.N.M. No. 56710. This species appears to be near *F. occidentalis* Walker but differs in the shape of the vertex, in tegminal markings, and in the genitalia.

Family ACANALONIIDAE

Genus ACANALONIA Spinola

Acanalonia SPINOLA, Ann. Soc. Ent. France, ser. 1, vol. 8, p. 447, 1839. (Genotype, *Acanalonia servillei* Spinola, *ibid.*, p. 448, pl. 16, fig. 2.)

Head, with eyes, as wide as pronotum; vertex short, more than twice as broad as long, not much produced in front of eyes, lateral margins subparallel, somewhat diverging distally, anterior margin transverse or convex, posterior margin broadly excavated; frons broader than long, median carina present, often feeble, lateral carinae present at base, usually obsolete on disk, lateral margins subparallel, curved inwards to frontoclypeal suture; clypeus devoid of carinae; antennae with second segment subglobular at apex, tapering basad, terminal segment with seta arising at apex on posteroventral side of rim. Pronotum short, approximately as long as vertex, impressed on each side of middle line, with median and lateral carinae feebly present or obsolete, anterior margin convex, posterior margin shallowly concave; mesonotum feebly carinate. Posttibiae unarmed. Tegmina with costal margin broadly rounded, apical margin rounded-truncate, commissural margin straight, basal stalk of M longer than basal cell, second fork of M level with middle of clavus.

ACANALONIA UMBELLICAUDA, new species

PLATE 16, FIGURES 493–502, 510

Male: Length, 8.0 mm.; tegmen, 8.5 mm. Female: Length, 7.9 mm.; tegmen, 9.7 mm.

Vertex 3.3 times as broad as long, anterior margin straight, carinae obsolete; frons broader than long (1.2:1), flattened, with median carina present throughout, lateral carinae present only at base.

Pale green; costa pallid, anterior margin of genae, protarsi and mesotarsi, and a row of short linear markings inside apical margin of tegmen fuscous, procoxae and mesocoxae fuscous speckled with whitish spots.

Anal segment of male large, narrow in dorsal view, produced on each side beyond anal opening into a large lobe, broadly triangular in side view and twice as long as preanal portion, with a notch near its base. Pygofer with lateral margins straight, ventral posterior border transverse, devoid of a process. Aedeagus tubular, a flattened bladelike process arising on each side at middle, directed posteriorly and slightly upward, expanding distally and truncate at apex with a short spine at one angle; a pair of slender spines arising at apex, curving ventrad and directed anteriorly for nearly whole length of aedeagus. Genital styles broad, dorsal margin convex, ventral margin straight, rounded apically, a small peglike process with a sclerotized tip on dorsal margin near base.

Anal segment of female elongate, produced beyond anal opening in a grooved lamina notched at apex. Ovipositor with lateral styles large, concave on dorsal margin, ventral margin curving through a quarter circle, greatest width 1.4 times length; first valvulae with a dorsal outer row of six small teeth near apex, and a longer inner row of five broader teeth. Pregenital sternite with hind margin sinuate, slightly produced near middle line, with a V-shaped notch medially.

Described from one male and three females collected by the writer at St. Augustine, Trinidad, B. W. I., on various dates between April 1942 and March 1943 on *Caesalpinia* and *Asparagus*. Holotype male in B.M.N.H.; allotype, U.S.N.M. No. 56711. This species is distinguished by its flat frons, by the shape of the anal segment of the male and of the aedeagus, by the shape of the lateral styles of the ovipositor, and by the fuscous-speckled protibiae and mesotibiae. It is very near the female type of *A. complanata* Walker, described from an unknown locality.

ACANALONIA THEOBROMAE, new species

PLATE 16, FIGURES 503–509, 511–513

Male: Length, 8.2 mm.; tegmen, 7.5 mm. Female: Length, 8.5 mm.; tegmen, 8.6 mm.

Vertex short, 2.5 times as broad as long, anterior margin somewhat angularly produced, apex rounded; frons wider than long (1.2:1), inflated medially at base, flat near suture, median carina feebly present, lateral carinae obsolete on disk.

Pale green; costa pallid, a series of minute linear markings inside apical margin of tegmen fuscous, protarsi and mesotarsi pale fuscous, protibiae distally pale fuscous speckled with white.

Anal segment of male long, narrow, tubular, postanal portion slightly deflexed, shorter than preanal portion (1:1.3), a slight protuberance ventrally below anal opening. Pygofer with posterior lateral margins slightly convex, ventral margin very slightly concave, devoid of a median process. Aedeagus tubular, with a membranous flange, slightly incurved, arising on dorsal margin in distal half and tapering to apex, a somewhat folded eminence on each side ventrally at middle from which arises a bladelike spine directed in its basal half mesad and posteriorly, and bent outward in its distal half; in middle line ventrally a single process in form of a broad short spine directed caudad. Anal segment of female elongate, produced beyond anal opening in a flat and shallowly grooved lamina scarcely notched at apex. Ovipositor with lateral styles large, bluntly angularly pointed, dorsal margin concave, ventral margin curved through less than a quarter of a circle, greatest width 1.6 times length; first valvulae with a double row of four teeth on dorsal margin and five teeth crowded near apex. Pregenital sternite with hind margin sinuate, slightly produced caudad on each side of middle line with a rather broad shallow emargination medially.

Egg ovoid, with a chorionic process at one pole tightly coiled, when extended consisting of a filament forking into two rami distally; length, 1.1 mm., width, 0.5 mm.

Described from four males and six females collected at St. Augustine, Trinidad, B. W. I., by the writer (May 13, Aug. 10, 25, Oct. 2, 1942) on *Hibiscus*, coffee, and cacao, and three females collected by Dr. E. McC. Callan (May 18, 1939, Feb. 8, 1943) on cacao in the same locality. Holotype male and allotype, U.S.N.M. No. 56712; paratype in B.M.N.H. This species is distinguished by the tumid frons, the curved anterior margin of the vertex, the shape of the anal segment of the male, and of the aedeagus, by the broad excavation on the hind margin of the pregenital sternite, and the shape of the lateral styles, and by the fuscous color of the distal half of the protibiae. It differs from *A. decens* Stål, to which it appears most nearly allied, in the more rounded apical angle of the tegmina.

Family ISSIDAE
Subfamily ISSINAE

15a. *Wings with apical margin entire, without a deep cleft; anal area not very large.*

Tribe ISSINI
UGOA, new genus

Head, with eyes, as broad as pronotum; vertex hollowed out, more than twice as broad as long in middle, lateral margins approximately parallel, anterior margin straight, transverse, carinate, posterior margin shallowly excavated, median carina absent or obsolete; frons longer than broad, slightly curved in profile, lateral margins expanding to below level of antennae, thence curved rather sharply inwards to suture, median carina present, lateral margins carinate, slightly raised; clypeus short, scarcely half as long as frons, devoid of lateral carinae, median carina present with an eminence at basal quarter; antennae with second segment somewhat longer than broad, devoid of perisensorial granulations on ventral surface, seta arising on ventral margin at apex of third segment. Pronotum short, depressed on disk, anterior margin convex, produced into emargination of vertex, anterior border of disk transverse, posterior margin angularly excavated, anterior margin slightly raised, posterior margin less so, median carina present, lateral carinae following line of hind border of eyes; mesonotum slightly broader than long, median carina distinct except at apex, lateral carinae joined to median carina anteriorly, diverging laterally and curving posteriorly, becoming obsolete before middle, scutellum acutely triangular. Posttibiae unarmed. Tegmina elongate, slightly tapering apically, common stalk Sc + R scarcely as long as basal cell, M forking about middle, Cu$_1$ forking just basad of apex of clavus, clavus long, its apex three-quarters of length of tegmen from base.

This genus comes nearest to *Colpoptera* Burmeister but differs in not having the costal margin sinuate or markedly narrowed distally, in the broadly rounded sutural angle, and in the proportionately shorter membrane distad of apex of clavus.

Genotype: *Ugoa glauca,* new species.

UGOA GLAUCA, new species
PLATE 16, FIGURES 514–518; PLATE 17, FIGURES 519–526

Male: Length, 4.6 mm.; tegmen, 5.3 mm. Female: Length, 4.9 mm.; tegmen, 6.0 mm.

Vertex broader than long (2.4 : 1) ; frons longer than broad (1.3 : 1).

Pale green, abdomen pallid green; middle line of vertex, pronotum, mesonotum, and abdominal tergites sometimes broadly pale fuscous; tegmina green, commissural margin narrowly pale fuscous, veins concolorous; wings hyaline, faintly clouded fuscous, veins concolorous, Cu$_2$ and anal veins fuscous.

Anal segment of male tubular, in profile expanding distally, postanal portion deflexed, equal in length to preanal portion, telson fingerlike, three-quarters as long as postanal portion of segment. Pygofer with sides very slightly sinuate, devoid ventrally of a median process on hind margin. Aedeagus U-shaped in profile, a pair of rather long spines ventrally near base directed posteriorly and ventrad; a broad bifurcate spine, with the upper limb shorter, arising near apex on each side and directed anteriorly; apex of aedeagus curved anteriorly, beaklike in profile, thin, with two short sclerotized thickenings visible inside. Genital styles broad, ventral margin longer than dorsal, upper margin almost straight, apical margin oblique, apical process in form of a broad slightly curved spine directed vertically.

Anal segment of female tubular, deflexed, postanal portion rather longer than preanal, telson long. Ovipositor with lateral styles broad, dorsal margin oblique, almost straight, ventral margin curved, strongly convex, apex narrowly membranous; first valvulae broad, with four small teeth and two larger apical teeth on dorsal margin. Pregenital sternite produced on hind margin in middle third, median area with margin straight, transverse.

Egg narrowly ovoid, more flattened on one side, a short clavate process directed obliquely upward from one pole, and from its base two narrow ridges, subparallel and approximated, passing along egg to opposite pole; length, 1.1 mm.; width, 0.2 mm.

Described from 13 males and 29 females collected by the writer near Santa Margarita, Trinidad, B. W. I. (May 4, 11, June 8, 1942, and subsequent dates), on *Cordia*, *Erythrina*, and fiddlewood. Holotype male and allotype, U.S.N.M. No. 56751; paratype in B.M.N.H.

15b. *Wings with apical margin cleft; anal area very large.*

Tribe THIONIINI

Genus THIONIA Stål

Thionia STÅL, Berliner Ent. Zeitschr., vol. 3, p. 321, 1859. (Genotype, *Issus longipennis* Spinola, designated by Van Duzee, Check list of Hemiptera of America north of Mexico, p. 81, 1916.)

Form rather broadly oval. Vertex broad, anterior margin transverse, curved, or even somewhat produced; frons broad, median carina usually present, lateral carinae present or obsolete, a series of pustules inside lateral margins. Pronotum short, anterior margin distinctly convex, lateral margins very short, posterior margin transverse, with a median notch; mesonotum short, less than combined length along middle line of vertex and pronotum, lateral margins strongly oblique, slightly sinuate, scutellum pointed at apex. Tegmina rather broad, costal margin distinctly rounded, commissural margin straight, apical margin strongly rounded, veins simple, Sc and R with a short common stalk at base, M branching before middle, a few transverse veins, especially distad of apex of clavus. Wings large, anal fold greatly dilated and separated from remainder of wing by a deep cleft in the apical margin.

THIONIA DRYAS, new species

PLATE 17, FIGURES 527-534

Male: Length, 5.1 mm.; tegmen, 5.3 mm.   Female: Length, 5.3 mm.; tegmen, 5.5 mm.

Vertex depressed, broader than long in middle (2.3:1), anterior margin transverse, very slightly angulate medially, basal margin shallowly excavate; frons slightly broader than long (1.1:1), slightly tumid laterally at apex, median carina somewhat swollen in basal quarter, obsolete at apex. Pronotum with median carina obsolete; mesonotum feebly tricarinate. Hind tibiae with two spines in apical half. Abdomen without paired eminences ventrally.

Testaceous, suffused with reddish brown; middle and lateral margins of frons, clypeus, a small suffusion at base of antennae, two triangular spots at apex of vertex, a triangular spot on each side of middle line of pronotum, and a crescentic mark on each lateral lobe, medial portion of abdominal sclerites, and a band near base and a second band near apex of profemora fuscous; eyes red, with a pale spot; tegmina yellowish, hyaline, mottled with pale fuscous, darker at base of Sc and M and near stigma, a broad irregular pale fuscous band from costal to commissural margin basad of humeral protuberance, an irregular line of rather large pallid spots obliquely from anterior margin in basal third to union of claval veins, a small pale spot at stigma, a distinct pale spot at junction of claval veins, and a pale spot on each side of anterior claval vein near base, transverse veins rather pallid. Wings smoky, veins concolorous, with narrow darker edges.

Anal segment of male short, postanal portion longer than preanal, in profile porrect and narrow. Aedeagus tubular, curved distally upwards and bending caudad at apex assuming a spoutlike appearance, a long spine ventrally on each side, arising about two-thirds from base, about half as long as aedeagus, curving anteriorly, giving off a small spine near middle of upper edge. Genital styles with ventral margin straight, dorsal margin sinuate, strongly bent upward distally, apical margin oblique, apical process of styles broad and blunt, bearing three small teeth.

Anal segment of female short, postanal portion semiovate. Ovipositor with lateral styles very broad basally, tapering rapidly to apex, which is subtriangular, rounded and incurved, membranous in texture; first valvulae broad at base, tapering distally, with four teeth on dorsal margin near apex. Pregenital sternite with hind margin slightly excavated medially.

Described from one male and one female collected by the writer on the Lalaja road, Northern Range, Trinidad, B. W. I. (May 29, 1936), at 2,500 feet in forest. Holotype male in B.M.N.H.; allotype female, U.S.N.M. No. 56752. This species is distinguished by the shape of the male genitalia and by the color pattern.

THIONIA MAMMIFERA, new species

PLATE 17, FIGURES 535–543

Female: Length, 6.0 mm.; tegmen, 6.5 mm.

Vertex broader than long (2 : 1), depressed, median carina feebly present; frons as broad as long in middle, median carina present, weak apically, lateral carinae obsolete. Hind tibiae with two spines before apex. Abdomen with a pair of papillate protuberances near middle line ventrally on sixth segment.

Testaceous-fuscous; vertex testaceous, an oblique pale fuscous band from middle line at apex to each lateral basal angle, frons mottled fuscous, clypeus testaceous banded fuscous, genae testaceous, a fuscous spot between ocelli and antennae; pronotum testaceous, a fuscous suffusion in middle of lateral lobes, mesonotum fuscous to piceous, carinae paler; legs and abdomen testaceous; tegmina brownish yellow, a pallid spot between M and Cu_1 level with R fork, the transverse veins and the apex of the external claval vein broadly pallid, a few small pale spots between claval veins near base; eyes red, with a pale crescentic band horizontally.

Anal segment short, postanal portion in dorsal view tapering, truncate at apex. Ovipositor with lateral styles broad at base, both margins convex, tapering subequally to a membranous lip at truncate apex; first valvulae broad, with two small subapical teeth and one larger flattened tooth at apex dorsally. Pregenital sternite with posterior margin sinuate, shallowly excavated medially, with a slight median groove basad of hind margin.

Egg bluntly fusiform, 0.9 mm. long, 0.5 mm. wide, with the surface finely reticulate.

Described from two females collected in Trinidad, B. W. I., by F. W. Urich (1923). Type, U.S.N.M. No. 56713. The writer has described this species, although no males were available, on account of the distinguishing characters of the singly banded eyes and the abdominal ventral protuberances.

THIONIA BUFO, new species

PLATE 17, FIGURES 544–554

Male: Length, 6.5 mm.; tegmen, 5.6 mm.   Female: Length, 7.1 mm.; tegmen, 5.9 mm.

Vertex broader than long in middle (3:1), devoid of median carina; frons slightly broader than long (1.1:1), very slightly rounded in profile, median carina present, lateral carinae obsolete. Pronotum and mesonotum without median carinae.

Pallid olive-testaceous; vertex mottled pale fuscous, a piceous spot at base of middle line, a distinct clear triangular area near each posterior lateral angle; frons sprinkled fuscous, clypeus pale basally, piceous at apex, rostrum pale; eyes red or mauve, with two faint vertical stripes anteriorly, genae pale, a dark spot between antennae and ocelli, antennae pale basally, second segment piceous; pronotum testaceous, a row of five small piceous spots on anterior margin at each side, lateral lobes sprinkled fuscous and with a piceous spot; mesonotum sprinkled with pale fuscous; legs pallid, slightly sprinkled fuscous; abdomen fuscous dorsally, sternites fuscous in middle, paler laterally; tegmina pale testaceous or pallid, a short irregular oblique fuscous band across humeral protuberance, a sparse fuscous mottling from stigma to middle of clavus, a second irregular band halfway between this and apical margin; wings smoky, veins broadly infuscate.

Anal segment of male shorter than genital styles, postanal portion slightly shorter than the preanal, apex sinuate. Aedeagus tubular, curved dorsad apically; a pair of flattened lobes, rounded at tip, arising at apex and directed anteriorly above aedeagus for two-thirds of its length, ventrolaterally two-thirds from base a pair of spines on each side, the outer spine filamentous, tapering, three-quarters as long as aedeagus, inner spine half length of former, flattened, narrowed, and sharply curved at tip, a folded membrane at apex of aedeagus. Genital styles in profile triangular, dorsal margin slightly curved, a short deflexed plate on dorsal margin near base, with two points distally, directed outward, and a thinner plate of equal length directed inward from margin. Pygofer with lateral margins sinuate, ventral posterior margin transverse, devoid of a median process.

Anal segment of female short, postanal portion twice as long as preanal, subovate. Ovipositor with lateral styles broad, subquadrate, with a membranous lip bordering the apical margin; first valvulae broad, ventral margin curved upward distally, dorsal margin straight with five small teeth and a larger tricuspidate tooth at apex, two small teeth ventrad of apex. Pregenital sternite with hind margin shallowly excavated.

Described from two males and two females taken by the writer at Santa Margarita, Trinidad, B. W. I. (March 12, 14, 1943), on the woody stem of a leguminous vine. Holotype male and allotype, U.S.N.M. No. 56714. This species is distinguished by the proportions of the vertex and frons, the shape of the genitalia of both sexes, and by the color.

1. *Bothriocera bicornis* (Fabricius): Tegmen.

2–10. *Pintalia albolineata* Muir: 2, Head and pronotum, dorsal view; 3, head in profile; 4, tegmen; 5, posterior view of anal segment and left genital style; 6, anal segment of female, side view; 7, same, dorsal view; 8, aedeagus, right side; 9, same, left side; 10, pygofer, genital style, and anal segment of male, side view.

11–16. *Pintalia straminea*, new species: 11, Head in profile; 12, apex of anal segment in male, dorsal view; 13, aedeagus, left side; 14, same, right side; 15, pygofer, genital style, and anal segment of male, side view; 16, pygofer and genital styles, ventral view.

17–26. *Mnemosyne arenae*, new species: 17, Pygofer and genital styles, ventral view; 18, pygofer, genital styles, and anal segment of male, side view; 19, aedeagus, ventral view; 20, same, left side; 21, anal segment of male, dorsal view; 22, anal segment of female, dorsal view; 23, head and pronotum, dorsal view; 24, head, frontal view; 25, aedeagus, right side; 26, tegmen.

27–36. *Oliarus biperforatus*, new species: 27, Head, pronotum, and mesonotum, dorsal view; 28, head, frontal view; 29, lateral margin of pygofer, left side; 30, anal segment of female, dorsal view; 31, anal segment of male, right side; 32, hind margin of pygofer and genital styles, ventral view; 33, genital style, right side; 34, aedeagus, ventral view; 35, same, right side; 36, tegmen.

37–41. *Oliarus opalinus*, new species: 37, Anal segment of female, dorsal view; 38, tegmen; 39, wing; 40, head and pronotum, dorsal view; 41, head, frontal view.

42–44. *Oliarus quadratus*, new species: 42, Head, dorsal view; 43, tegmen; 44, anal segment of female, dorsal view.

45–54. *Oliarus maidis*, new species: 45, Aedeagus, left side; 46, same, dorsal view; 47, anal segment of male, dorsal view; 48, genital style, side view; 49, medioventral process of pygofer, ventral view; 50, anal segment of female, dorsal view; 51, head, pronotum, and mesonotum, dorsal view; 52, head, frontal view; 53, tegmen; 54, wing.

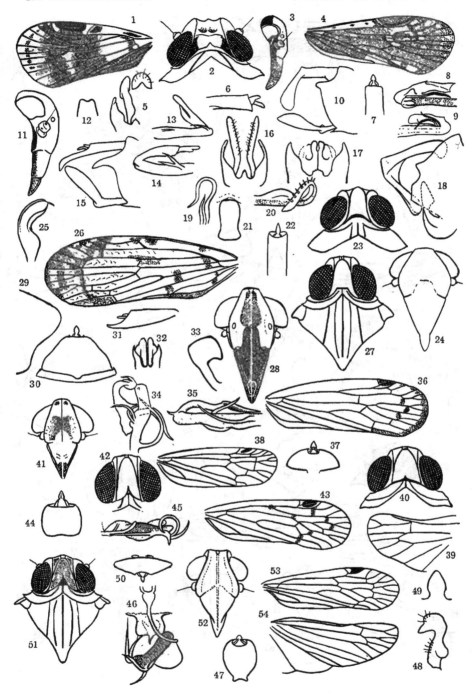

FULGOROIDEA FROM TRINIDAD

SEE OPPOSITE PAGE FOR EXPLANATION

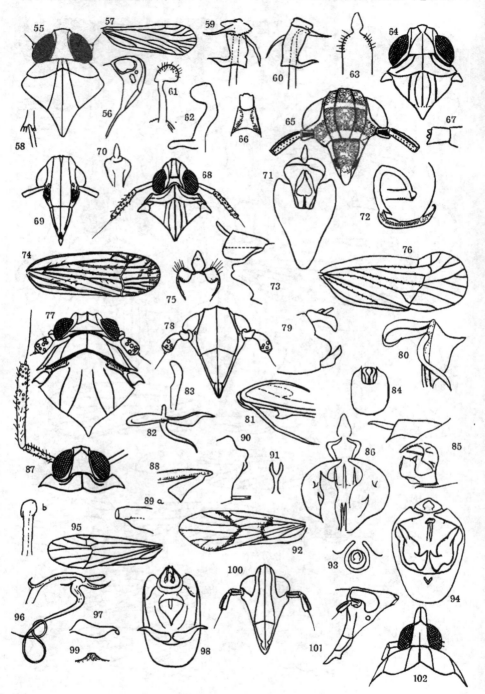

FULGOROIDEA FROM TRINIDAD

PLATE 8

55–63. *Paramyndus cocois,* new species: 55, Head, pronotum, and mesonotum, dorsal view; 56, head in profile; 57, tegmen; 58, spines at apex of posttibia; 59, aedeagus, left side; 60, same, right side; 61, genital style, ventral view; 62, same, side view; 63, anal segment of male, dorsal view.

64–67. *Pentagramma bivittata* Crawford: 64, Head, pronotum, and mesonotum, dorsal view; 65, head, frontal view; 66, anal segment of female, dorsal view; 67, same, side view.

68–74. *Eucanyra flagellata,* new species: 68, Head, pronotum, and mesonotum, dorsal view; 69, head, frontal view; 70, anal segment of male, dorsal view; 71, pygofer, genital styles, and apex of anal segment of male, posteroventral view; 72, aedeagus, left side; 73, pygofer and anal segment of male, right side (left in transparency); 74, tegmen.

75–84. *Tetrasteira albitarsis,* new species: 75, Anal segment of male, posterior view; 76, tegmen; 77, head, pronotum, and mesonotum, dorsal view; 78, head, frontal view; 79, pygofer, anal segment of male, and genital style, left side; 80, aedeagus, ventral view; 81, same, right side; 82, same, posterior view; 83, genital style, ventral view; 84, pygofer and genital styles, posteroventral view.

85, 86. *Burnilia spinifera,* new species: 85, Pygofer, genital style, and anal segment of male, side view; 86, pygofer, left genital style, and anal segment, ventral view.

87–94. *Malaxa gracilis,* new species: 87, Head and pronotum, dorsal view (right antenna not shown); 88, penis, left side; 89, penis, right side (*a*) and ventral view (*b*); 90, pygofer, left side; 91, median ventral process of pygofer, ventral view; 92, tegmen; 93, anal segment of male, posterodorsal view; 94, pygofer, genital styles, and anal segment, posterior view.

95–102. *Saccharosydne saccharivora* (Westwood): 95, Tegmen; 96, penis, left side; 97, right genital style, posterior view; 98, pygofer, genital styles, and anal segment, posterior view; 99, middle of hind margin of pygofer, ventral view; 100, head, frontal view; 101, head in profile; 102, head and pronotum, dorsal view.

511

PLATE 9

103–106. *Delphacodes pallidivitta*, new species: 103, Penis, left side (*a*) and right side (*b*); 104, penis, ventral view (posterior spines in transparency); 105, armature of diaphragm; 106, pygofer, genital styles, and anal segment, posterior view.

107–110. *Delphacodes axonopi*, new species: 107, Pygofer, genital styles, and anal segment, posterior view; 108, penis, left side; 109, penis, right side; 110, genital style, side view.

111–114. *Delphacodes spinigera*, new species: 111, Pygofer, genital styles, and anal segment, posterior view; 112, lateral margin of pygofer, left side; 113, penis, right side; 114, head and pronotum, dorsal view.

115. *Delphacodes teapae* (Fowler): Pygofer, genital styles, and anal segment, posterior view,

116, 117. *Sogata furcifera* (Horváth): 116, Pygofer, genital styles, and anal segment, posterior view; 117, penis, right side.

118–123. *Derbe uliginosa*, new species: 118, Pregenital sternite of female, ventral view; 119, tegmen; 120, anal segment of female, dorsal view; 121, ovipositor and anal segment, left side; 122, first valvula of ovipositor, upper lobe; 123, same, ventral lobe.

124–128. *Derbe boletophila*, new species: 124, Tegmen; 125, aedeagus, right side; 126, same, left side; 127, right genital style, ventral view; 128, anal segment of male, lateral margin of pygofer, and genital style, side view.

129–135. *Derbe semifusca*, new species: 129, Right genital style and ventral margin of pygofer, ventral view; 130; aedeagus, dorsal view; 131, same, right side; 132, same, left side; 133, genital style, left side (*a*) ornaméntation of dorsal margin, side view; 134, tegmen; 135, head, frontal view.

136–150. *Mysidia cinerea*, new species: 136, Tegmen; 137, apex of aedeagus, left side; 138, aedeagus, right side; 139, same, left side; 140, anal segment of male and right genital style, side view; 141, ornamentation on dorsal border of genital style, side view; 142, genital style and medial portion of pygofer, ventral view; 143, anal segment of male, dorsal view; 144, posterior ventral process on pregenital sternite of female, ventral view; 145, anal segment of female, ovipositor, and pregenital plate, side view; 146, first valvula of ovipositor, right side, side view; 147, head, dorsal view (left antenna not shown); 148, antenna, frontal view; 149, egg, side view; 150, egg, end view.

151–157. *Omolicna proxima*, new species: 151, Aedeagus, right side; 152, same, left side; 153, same, ventral view; 154, genital styles and medioventral process of pygofer, ventral view; 155, right lateral style, side view; 156, first valvula of ovipositor, left side, side view; 157, posterior margin of pregenital sternite of female.

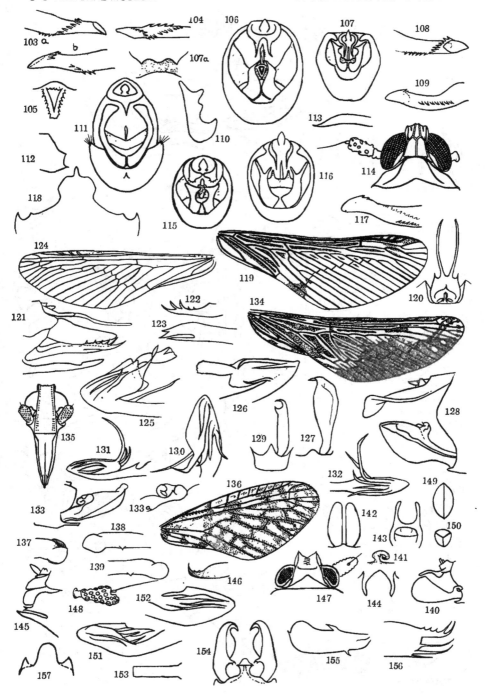

FULGOROIDEA FROM TRINIDAD
SEE OPPOSITE PAGE FOR EXPLANATION

FULGOROIDEA FROM TRINIDAD

SEE OPPOSITE PAGE FOR EXPLANATION

PLATE 10

158–160. *Omolicna proxima,* new species: 158, Head, dorsal view; 159, head frontal view; 160, anal segment of male, side view.

161–168. *Omolicna rubrimarginata,* new species: 161, Head, dorsal view; 162, pygofer, ventral view; 163, lateral style of ovipositor, side view; 164, aedeagus, left side; 165, left genital style, side view; 166, anal segment of male, side view; 167, posterior lobe of pregenital sternite of female, ventral view; 168, right genital style of male, ventral view.

169–181. *Neocenchrea gregaria,* new species: 169, Aedeagus, ventral view; 170, same, right side, posterior lobe extended caudad; 171, posterior margin of pygofer and right genital style, ventral view; 172, anal segment of male and right genital style, side view; 173, lateral styles of ovipositor, ventral view; 174, anal segment of female, lateral style, and first valvula of right side, side view; 175, lateral styles, posterior view; 176, first valvula, left side, side view; 177, posterior margin of pregenital sternite of female, ventral view; 178, egg, side view; 179, head, pronotum, and mesonotum, dorsal view; 180, tegmen; 181, head in profile.

182–190. *Cedusa cyanea,* new species: 182, Anal segment of male and right genital style, side view; 183, aedeagus, right side; 184, same, left side; 185, anal segment of female, dorsal view; 186, same, first valvula of left side, side view; 187, lateral style of ovipositor, lateroventral view; 188, head, anterolateral view; 189, tegmen; 190, head and pronotum, dorsal view.

191–194. *Cedusa rubriventris,* new species: 191, Aedeagus, right side; 192, same, left side; 193, left genital style of male, ventral view; 194, anal segment of male, dorsal view.

195–201. *Patara trigona,* new species: 195, Head, frontal view; 196, second joint of antenna, dorsal view; 197, aedeagus, dorsal view; 198, same, left side; 199, same, posterior view; 200, anal segment of male, dorsal view; 201, left genital style, left half of pygofer, and aedeagus, ventral view.

202–207. *Patara vittatipennis,* new species: 202, Tegmen; 203, antenna, dorsal view; 204, left genital style, side view; 205, same, left half of pygofer, ventral view; 206, aedeagus, right side; 207, same, left side.

208–213. *Patara poeciloptera,* new species: 208, Tegmen; 209, head, frontal view; 210, right genital style, side view; 211, aedeagus, left side; 212, right genital style, right side of pygofer, and aedeagus, ventral view; 213, anal segment of male and posterolateral margin of pygofer, side view.

513

PLATE 11

214. *Patara poeciloptera*, new species: Head in profile.

215–220. *Eparmenoides ripalis*, new species: 215, Head, frontal view; 216, tegmen; 217, wing; 218, anal segment of male, aedeagus, and right genital style, side view; 219, pregenital sternite of female, ventral view; 220, lateral style of ovipositor, left side.

221–229. *Bytrois nemoralis*, new species: 221, Head, frontal view; 222, right genital style of male, side view; 223, anal segment of female, side view; 224, aedeagus, left side; 225, anal segment of male, dorsal view; 226, lateral style of ovipositor, left side; 227, aedeagus, dorsal view; 228, tegmen; 229, wing.

230–234. *Lappida* sp. (?): 230, Tegmen; 231, first valvula of ovipositor, right side; 232, lateral style of ovipositor, right side; 233, anal segment of female, side view; 234, second valvula of ovipositor, right side.

235–238. *Hyalodictyon truncatum* (Walker): 235, Lateral style of ovipositor, right side, side view; 236, first valvula of ovipositor, right side; 237, head and pronotum, dorsal view; 238, anal segment of female, side view.

239–242. *Hyalodictyon fallax*, new species: 239, Head and pronotum, dorsal view; 240, right lateral style of ovipositor, side view; 241, right first valvula of ovipositor, side view; 242, anal segment of female, side view.

243–250. *Toropa ferrifera* (Walker): 243, Anal segment of female, side view; 244, right lateral style of ovipositor, side view; 245, second valvula of ovipositor, right side; 246, right valvula of ovipositor, side view; 247, head in profile; 248, pregenital sternite of female, side view; 249, head, dorsal (*a*) and side (*b*) views; 250, aedeagus, left side.

251–264. *Retiala viridis*, new species: 251, Head, frontal view; 252, head and pronotum, dorsal view; 253, head in profile; 254, aedeagus, with ventral lobe removed, ventral view; 255, ventral lobe of periandrium; 256, basal collar and ventral lobe of part of aedeagus; 257, anal segment of male, posterior margin of pygofer, and right genital style; 258, second segment of antenna, lateroventral view; 259, penis, right side; 260, periandrium, side view of right side; 261, lateral style of ovipositor, side view; 262, second valvula of ovipositor, side view; 263, first valvula of ovpositor, side view; 264, tegmen.

265–271. *Taosa vitrata* (Fabricius): 265, Head and pronotum, dorsal view; 266, head, frontal view; 267, tegmen; 268, anal segment of female, side view; 269, aedeagus, left side; 270, same, ventral view; 271, left genital style, side view.

272–274. *Taosa bimaculifrons* Muir: 272, Head and pronotum, dorsal view; 273, head, frontal view; 274, second valvula, left side.

514

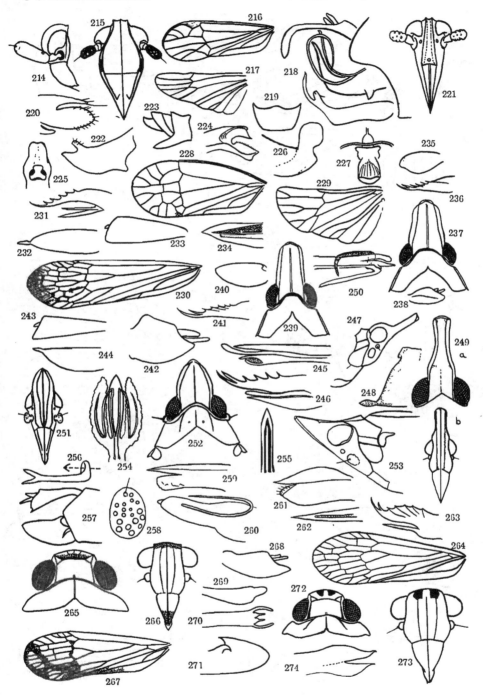

FULGOROIDEA FROM TRINIDAD
SEE OPPOSITE PAGE FOR EXPLANATION .

PROCEEDINGS, VOL. 95 PLATE 12

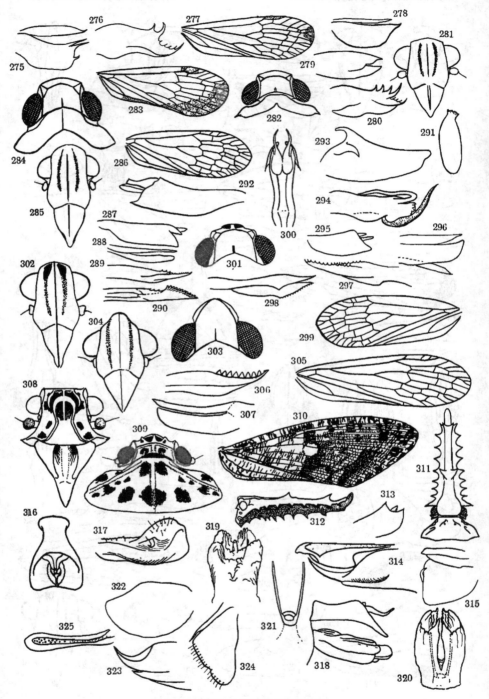

FULGOROIDEA FROM TRINIDAD

SEE OPPOSITE PAGE FOR EXPLANATION

PLATE 12

275–277. *Taosa bimaculifrons* Muir: 275, Left lateral style, side view; 276, first valvula of left side, side view; 277, tegmen.

278–283. *Taosa muliebris* (Walker): 278, Left lateral style of ovipositor, side view; 279, second valvula, left side; 280, first valvula of ovipositor, left side, side view; 281, head, frontal view; 282, head and pronotum, dorsal view; 283, tegmen.

284–291. *Taosa amazonica,* new species: 284, Head and pronotum, dorsal view; 285, head, frontal view; 286, tegmen (this is proportionately longer than shown in the figure); 287, anal segment of female, side view; 288, second valvula of ovipositor, left side view; 289, first valvula of ovipositor, left side view; 290, same, ventral view; 291, egg, side view.

292–302. *Taosa herbida* (Walker): 292, Anal segment of male, side view; 293, left genital style, side view; 294, aedeagus, left side; 295, anal segment of female, side view; 296, left lateral style of ovipositor, side view; 297, right first valvula of ovipositor, side view; 298, left second valvula of ovipositor, side view; 299, tegmen (this is proportionately longer than shown in figure); 300, aedeagus, ventral view; 301, head, dorsal view; 302, head, frontal view.

303–307. *Taosa paraherbida* Muir: 303, Head, dorsal view; 304, head, frontal view; 305, tegmen; 306, left first valvula of ovipositor, side view; 307, right lateral style, side view.

308–310. *Phenax variegata* (Olivier): 308, Head, frontal view; 309, head and pronotum, dorsal view; 310, tegmen.

311–315. *Cathedra serrata* (Fabricius): 311, Head and pronotum, dorsal view; 312, head in profile; 313, anal segment of female, ventrolateral view; 314, first and second valvulae of ovipositor, right side, side view; 315, lateral style of ovipositor, right side, with tip of first valvula projecting.

316–325. *Laternaria* spp.: 316, Anal segment of male, dorsal view; 317, left genital style, side view; 318, anal segment of male and left side of aedeagus, side view; 319, periandrium, dorsal view; 320, aedeagus, ventral view (penis in transparency); 321, penis, posteroventral view; 322, anal segment of female, side view; 323, first valvula of ovipositor, right side, side view; 324, right lateral style of ovipositor, side view; 325, second valvula of ovipositor, right side.

PLATE 13

326–329. *Scaralis semilimpida* (Walker): 326, Head and pronotum, dorsal view; 327, head, frontal view; 328, right lateral style of ovipositor, side view; 329, first and second valvulae of ovipositor, right side, side view (displaced).

330–335. *Ateson consimile*, new species: 330, Head and pronotum, dorsal view; 331, head, frontal view; 332, head in profile; 333, right lateral style of ovipositor, side view; 334, dorsal lobe of right first valvula of ovipositor, side view; 335, tegmen.

336–343. *Plectoderes collaris* (Fabricius): 336 Ventral lobe below first valvula of ovipositor, ventral view; 337, left lateral style of ovipositor, side view; 338, anal segment of female, dorsal view; 339, left second valvula of ovipositor, side view; 340, right·first valvula of ovipositor, with ventral lobe, side view; 341, head, pronotum, and mesonotum, dorsal view; 342, head, frontal view; 343, head in profile.

344–351. *Koloptera callosa* Metcalf: 344, Head, pronotum, and mesonotum, dorsal view; 345, head, frontal view; 346, tegmen; 347, aedeagus: *a*, periandrium, dorsal view; *b*, periandrium, ventral view; *c*, medioventral process of pygofer; *d*, apex of one of penial arms, side view; 348, right genital style, viewed laterally on inner face; 349, left lateral style of ovipositor, side view; 350, left first valvula of ovipositor, side view; 351, posterior margin of pregenital sternite of female, ventral view.

352–361. *Catonia pallida*, new species: 352, Head, pronotum, and mesonotum, dorsal view; 353, head, frontal view; 354, ventral lobe lying below first valvula of ovipositor, ventral view; 355, left lateral style of ovipositor, side view; 356, right first valvula of ovipositor and ventral lobe, side view; 357, right second valvula of ovipositor, side view; 358, second valvulae of ovipositor, dorsal view; 359, anal segment of female, dorsal view; 360, wing; 361, tegmen.

362–368. *Catonia pallidistigma*, new species: 362, Head and pronotum, dorsal view; 363, head, frontal view; 364, tegmen; 365, wing; 366, ventral lobe lying below first valvula of ovipositor, ventral view; 367, right lateral style of ovipositor, side view; 368, right first valvula of ovipositor, side view.

369–374. *Opsiplanon ornatifrons*, new species: 369, Right first valvula of ovipositor, side view; 370, right lateral style of ovipositor, side view; 371, same, posterior view; 372, ventral lobe lying below first valvula of ovipositor, ventral view, 373, head, pronotum, and mesonotum, dorsal view; 374, head, frontal view.

516

PROCEEDINGS, VOL 95 PLATE 13

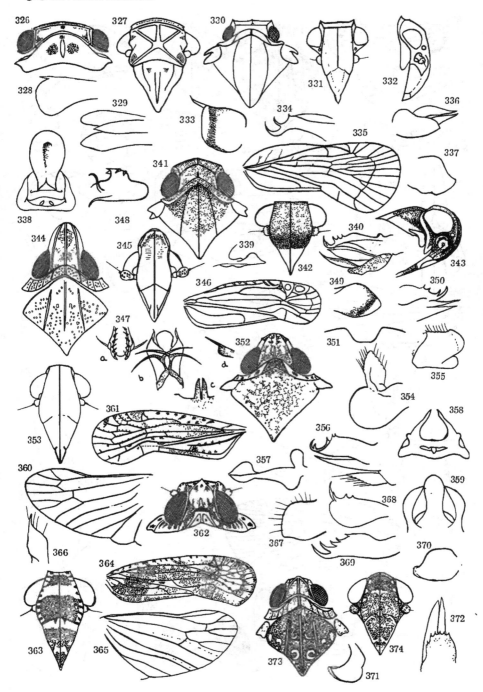

FULGOROIDEA FROM TRINIDAD

SEE OPPOSITE PAGE FOR EXPLANATION

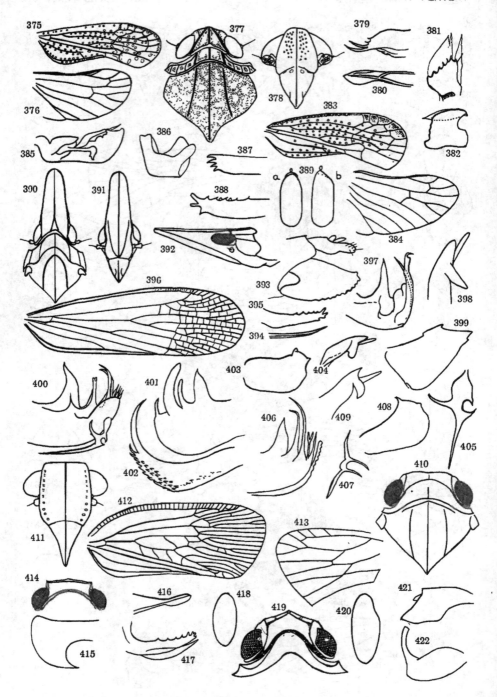

FULGOROIDEA FROM TRINIDAD
SEE OPPOSITE PAGE FOR EXPLANATION

PLATE 14

375, 376. *Opsiplanon ornatifrons,* new species: 375, Tegmen; 376, wing.

377–384. *Opsiplanon nemorosus,* new species: 377, Head, pronotum, and mesonotum, dorsal view; 378, head, frontal view; 379, dorsal lobe of right first valvula of ovipositor, side view; 380, right second valvula of ovipositor, side view; 381, left ventral lobe lying below first valvula of ovipositor, ventral view; 382, right lateral style of ovipositor, side view; 383, tegmen; 384, wing.

385–389. *Alcestis vitrea,* new species: 385, Aedeagus, left side; 386, left side of periandrium, side view; 387, right lateral style of ovipositor, side view; 388, right first valvula of ovipositor, side view; 389, egg, frontal (*a*) and side (*b*) views.

390–396. *Roesma grandis,* new species: 390, Head, pronotum, and mesonotum, dorsal view; 391, head, frontal view; 392, head in profile; 393, anal segment of female and left lateral style of ovipositor, side view; 394, left second valvula of ovipositor, side view; 395, left first valvula of ovipositor, side view; 396, tegmen.

397–399. *Bladina fuscovenosa* Stål: 397, Left side of aedeagus, side view; 398, anal segment of male, side view; 399, left genital style, side view.

400–405. *Bladina fuscana* Stål: 400, Left side of aedeagus, side view; 401, right side of periandrium, side view; 402, right side of penis, side view; 403, left genital style, side view; 404, anal segment of male, side view; 405, pendent spine of aedeagus, posterior view.

406–413. *Bladina rudis* (Walker): 406, Left side of aedeagus, side view; 407, pendent spine of aedeagus, posterior view; 408, left genital style, side view; 409, anal segment of male, side view; 410, head, pronotum, and mesonotum, dorsal view; 411, head, frontal view; 412, tegmen (distal cross veins omitted); 413, wing (anteroapical portion only).

414–418. *Nogodina reticulata* (Fabricius): 414, Head, dorsal view; 415, right lateral style, side view; 416, left second valvula of ovipositor, side view; 417, left first valvula of ovipositor, side view; 418, egg, side view.

419–422. *Biolleyana costalis* (Fowler): 419, Head and pronotum, dorsal view; 420, egg, side view; 421, anal segment of male, side view; 422, right genital style, side view.

PLATE 15

423–432. *Biolleyana costalis* (Fowler): 423, Dorsal process of aedeagus, right side, dorsolateral view; 424, lateral outer process of aedeagus, side view; 425, lateral inner process of aedeagus, side view; 426, lateroventral process of aedeagus, side view; 427, aedeagus, right side, side view; 428, head, frontal view; 429, wing; 430, tegmen; 431, first valvula of ovipositor, right side, viewed on inner face; 432, left lateral style of ovipositor, side view.

433–440. *Varciopsis tenguelana*, new species: 433, Head and pronotum, dorsal view; 434, head, frontal view; 435, wing; 436, tegmen; 437, anal segment of male, side view; 438, genital style of right side, side view; 439, aedeagus, right side, side view; 440, aedeagus, ventral view.

441–446. *Carthaeomorpha breviceps* Melichar: 441, Head in profile; 442, left second valvula of ovipositor, side view; 443, left first valvula of ovipositor, side view; 444, anal segment of female, left lateral style, side view; 445, head, dorsal view; 446, egg, side (*a*) and frontal (*b*) views.

447–454. *Epormenis aripensis*, new species: 447, Head, pronotum, and mesonotum, dorsal view; 448, head, frontal view; 449, anal segment of male, side view; 450, right side of aedeagus, side view; 451, right genital style, side view; 452, ventral processes of aedeagus, ventral view; 453, egg, side view; 454, egg, frontal view.

455–463. *Flatormenis squamulosa* (Fowler): 455, Anal segment of male, side view; 456, left side of aedeagus, side view; 457, aedeagus, ventral view; 458, left genital style, side view; 459, apex of right apical limb of penis, side view; 460, egg, frontal (*a*) and side (*b*) views; 461, left second valvula of ovipositor, side view; 462, penis, ventral view; 463, head, frontal view.

464. *Epormenis unimaculata* (Fennah): Aedeagus, ventral view.

465–469. *Anadascalia meridionalis*, new species: 465, Head, frontal (*a*) and dorsal (*b*) views; 466, head and pronotum in profile; 467, wing; 468, left lateral style of ovipositor, viewed laterally on inner face; 469, left first valvula of ovipositor, side view.

470–472. *Locrona nigrospersa* (Fennah): 470, Egg, side view; 471, left second valvula of ovipositor, side view; 472, apex of left limb of penis, side view (shown inverted).

473. *Poekilloptera phalaenoides* (Linnaeus): Egg, frontal view.

518

PROCEEDINGS, VOL. 95   PLATE 15

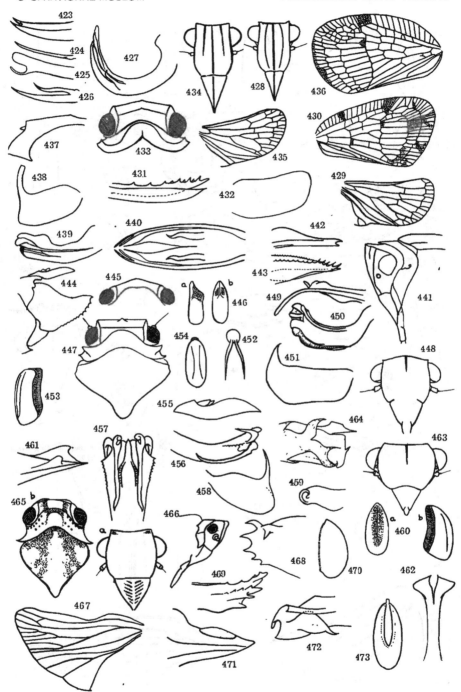

FULGOROIDEA FROM TRINIDAD
SEE OPPOSITE PAGE FOR EXPLANATION

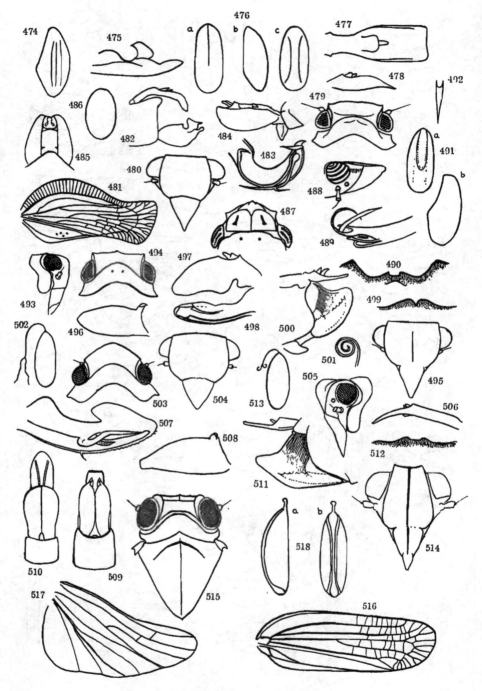

FULGOROIDEA FROM TRINIDAD

PLATE 16

474. *Poekilloptera phalaenoides* (Linnaeus): Egg, side view.

475. *Ormenis antoniae* Melichar: Left second valvula of ovipositor, side view.

476–478. *Epormenis fuliginosa* (Fennah): 476, Egg, frontal (*a*), side (*b*), and posterior (*c*) views; 477, anal segment of male, dorsal view; 478, same, side view.

479–486. *Euhyloptera corticalis,* new species: 479, Head and pronotum, dorsal view; 480, head, frontal view; 481, tegmen; 482, anal segment of male, left genital style, and hind margin of pygofer, side view; 483, left side of aedeagus, side view; 484, anal segment of female and right lateral style of ovipositor, side view; 485, anal segment of female, dorsal view; 486, egg, side view.

487–492. *Flatoidinus cordiae,* new species: 487, Head, dorsal view; 488, head, anterior portion in profile; 489, right side of aedeagus, side view; 490, posterior margin of pregenital sternite of female; 491, egg, frontal (*a*) and side (*b*) views; 492, ventral median part of periandrium, ventral view.

493–502, 510. *Acanalonia umbellicauda,* new species: 493, Head and pronotum in profile; 494, same, dorsal view; 495, head, frontal view; 496, right genital style, side view; 497, anal segment of male, side view; 498, right side of aedeagus, side view; 499, median portion of posterior margin of pregenital segment of female, ventral view; 500, anal segment of female and left lateral style of ovipositor, side view; 501, chorionic polar process of egg, slightly uncoiled, side view; 502, egg with chorionic process artificially uncoiled, side view; 510, pygofer, genital styles, and apex of anal segment, ventral view.

503–509, 511–513. *Acanalonia theobromae,* new species: 503, Head and pronotum, dorsal view; 504, head, frontal view; 505, head in profile; 506, anal segment of male, side view; 507, left side of aedeagus, side view; 508, right genital style, side view; 509, pygofer, genital styles, and apical part of anal segment, ventral view; 511, anal segment of female and right lateral style, side view; 512, posterior margin of pregenital segment of female, ventral view; 513, egg, side view.

514–518. *Ugoa glauca,* new species: 514, Head, frontal view; 515, head, pronotum, and mesonotum, dorsal view; 516, tegmen; 517, wing; 518, egg, side (*a*) and frontal (*b*) views.

PLATE 17

519–526. *Ugoa glauca,* new species: 519, Anal segment of male, side view; 520, aedeagus, left side; 521, left genital style, side view; 522, posterior margin of pygofer, ventral view; 523, anal segment of female and left lateral style, side view; 524, posterior margin of pregenital sternite, ventral view; 525, left first valvula of ovipositor, side view; 526, head in profile.

527–534. *Thionia dryas,* new species: 527, Head, frontal view; 528, head, pronotum, and mesonotum, dorsal view; 529, tegmen; 530, apex of right lateral style of ovipositor, showing extent of membranous area; 531, anal segment of male, side view; 532, left side of aedeagus, side view; 533, aedeagus, ventral view; 534, left genital style, viewed slightly dorsolaterally.

535–543. *Thionia mammifera,* new species: 535, Head, frontal view; 536, head and pronotum, dorsal view; 537, head in profile; 538, anal segment of female, side view; 539, left lateral style of ovipositor, side view; 540, ventral portion of sixth abdominal segment, viewed slightly ventrolaterally; 541, posterior margin of pregenital sternite of female, ventral view; 542, tegmen; 543, egg, side view.

544–554. *Thionia bufo,* new species: 544, Head, frontal view; 545, head, pronotum, and mesonotum, dorsal view; 546, tegmen; 547, wing; 548, pygofer and genital styles, ventral view; 549, anal segment of male, side view; 550, right side of aedeagus, side view; 551, right genital style, side view; 552, anal segment of female and left lateral style of ovipositor, side view; 553, left first valvula of ovipositor, side view; 554, posterior margin of pregenital sternite of female, ventral view.

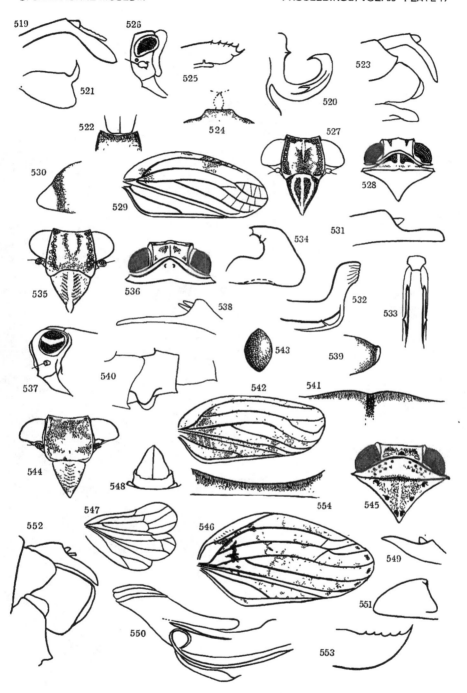

CPSIA information can be obtained
at www.ICGtesting.com
Printed in the USA
BVHW092245080922
646639BV00008B/108